THE 411

SPIRIT-FILLED HANDBOOK

THINGS I WISH I KNEW AS A NEW CHRISTIAN

A BOOK OF TESTIMONIES & HELPFUL TIPS

WRITTEN BY
B.A. GIBSON

authorbagibson@yahoo.com

Find me on Facebook: Author B.A. Gibson.

C000091557

Trilogy Christian Publishers
A Wholly Owned Subsidiary of Trinity Broadcasting Network
2442 Michelle Drive
Tustin, CA 92780
Copyright © 2023 by B.A. Gibson.

All Scripture quotations, unless otherwise noted, are taken from The Holy Bible, English Standard Version. ESV® Text Edition: 2016. Copyright © 2001 by Crossway Bibles, a publishing ministry of Good News Publishers.

Scripture quotations marked AMP are taken from the Amplified Bible Copyright © 1954, 1958, 1962, 1964, 1965, 1987 by The Lockman Foundation, La Habra, CA 90631. All rights reserved. For Permission to Quote Information visit http://www.lockman.org.

Scripture quotations marked ASV are taken from the American Standard Version of the Bible. Public domain.

Scripture quotations marked (NIV) are taken from THE HOLY BIBLE, NEW INTERNATIONAL VERSION®, NIV® Copyright © 1973, 1978, 1984, 2011 by Biblica, Inc.® Used by permission. All rights reserved worldwide.

Scripture quotations marked NKJV are taken from the New King James Version®. Copyright © 1982 by Thomas Nelson. Used by permission. All rights reserved.

Scripture quotations marked NRSV are taken from the New Revised Standard Version Updated Edition. Copyright © 2021 National Council of Churches of Christ in the United States of America. Used by permission. All rights reserved worldwide.

Scripture quotations marked KJV are taken from the King James Version of the Bible. Public domain.

All rights reserved, including the right to reproduce this book or portions thereof in any form whatsoever. For information, address Trilogy Christian Publishing
Rights Department, 2442 Michelle Drive, Tustin, Ca 92780.
Trilogy Christian Publishing/ TBN and colophon are trademarks of Trinity Broadcasting Network.
For information about special discounts for bulk purchases, please contact Trilogy Christian Publishing.

Trilogy Disclaimer: The views and content expressed in this book are those of the author and may not necessarily reflect the views and doctrine of Trilogy Christian Publishing or the Trinity Broadcasting Network.

10 9 8 7 6 5 4 3 2 1
Library of Congress Cataloging-in-Publication Data is available.
ISBN 979-8-89041-469-4
ISBN 979-8-89041-470-0 (ebook)

To my loving and supportive family, my husband, John, my beautiful children, grandchildren, brothers and sisters, my mom, dad, and stepmom. All of you are the reason I am who I am and why I persevere to reach my goals. I love you all with my whole heart. Thank you for loving me. Follow Jesus. He will never lead you on the wrong path.

To my sister in Christ, Cris. I am looking forward to celebrating our Lord together in heaven. I miss you every day.

To my readers… I pray you walk away with a newfound love and hunger for our Savior, Jesus Christ.

To my Jesus, all of You and none of me, my Lord.

FOREWORD

Do you know who you are? Deep down. Are you searching for answers? Are you a Christian? Not sure? Do you walk through your daily Christian life with the knowledge, strength, and fortitude afforded to us by Jesus? Or do you walk hoping, but not quite sure what, where, or how it's going to work out?

That was me. Baptized a Catholic girl, I knew not of this Jesus and His beautiful relationship skills or of the detail and intricate love and giftings He bestowed upon us. I walked through life, knowing I needed God in times of trouble but not so much any other time. And life was there with its ups, downs, in-betweens...meh.

This is it. This is the answer to the question I didn't even know I needed an answer to. I didn't know. I didn't even know the question. I had no idea that I was in need of something, except for a few weird occurrences in my past I might want to know about. Why is the world the way it is? A life lived, my beautiful kids, work, school, and so forth, but just hangin' in there. Dealing with troubles like divorce and bills, with my strong and not-so-strong moments.

But here we are. With some answers. Not all, but some. Psalm 46 says, "God is our refuge and strength, a very present help in trouble." So when our world is shaken, and even when it's not, He is there. He promises. We all need to be aware of that and so much more.

Whether you have just found Jesus or He has just found you, or you're curious, this book will walk you through some of the needs, some of the answers, and some of the things I wish I would have known more of in my walk earlier in life.

REFERENCES/ACKNOWLEDGEMENTS/ THANK YOU TO:

Charles Capps Ministries

Jesse Duplantis Ministries

Andrew Wommack Ministries

biblegateway.com

biblehub.com

Pastor Dawn Young

Abundant Life Church in LaSalle, IL

Pastors Chico and Jane Perez

Reverend Kevin Ashby and Ann Ashby

My Sister In Christ, Cris Westfall

Send your inquiries and prayer requests to our Author at authorbagibson@yahoo.com.

Find this author on Facebook: Author B.A.Gibson.

CONTENTS

CHAPTER 1

BORN AGAIN? (YOU MEAN BIBLE
THUMPER, HOLY ROLLER?)

Yes, I know, but really, if you weren't brought up in an evangelical or saved family environment, you thought it too. I too, believed that outside of my demure, closed-minded, religious attitude that "those people" were strange and geeky and just weird. Any church that was not structured as the one I attended occasionally and on holidays was just not my "cup of tea."

It began when my grandchildren were going to be dedicated at a church my daughter and her husband attended. Of course we went. It wasn't the building, which was an old party hall turned into a church, that pulled me. It was the atmosphere. Everyone was kind and welcoming, of course. But there was something there that made me feel like I was home. Warm, loving, accepted. Beautiful. The Holy Spirit. It was the Holy Spirit surrounding and loving us. We didn't know.

After an exhilarating message and ceremony for the kids, I didn't want to leave. My husband, the "walls will fall and burn if I go" kind of guy, didn't want to leave. We couldn't wait to return. People were so interested in us and made us feel welcome. One in particular was a special, loving lady who very soon became my best friend and mentor, Cris.

Well, long story short, I fell in love with Jesus. I read and studied THE BIBLE! I asked Jesus into my heart and life and became a born-again believer. The more I heard about Jesus and His walk on earth and His sacrifice and why He did it—ohhhh, I

2

just couldn't get enough. I still can't. And I was learning WHO I was.

That's it, you know. To be born again means you ask Jesus to be your Lord and Savior. You ask for forgiveness for any sins, and tell Him you believe He died on the Cross and was resurrected to save us. It's the only way to heaven. Jesus told us in John 3:3 "Most assuredly, I say to you, unless one is born again, he cannot see the kingdom of God." It's a confession of your belief and out loud request for Jesus in your life—from your heart.

And by the way, for anyone who knows the Catholic faith, the Apostles Creed is similar in the confession of beliefs but without asking Jesus into your heart and life.

So, there I was, "on fire," so they call it, for the Lord. Something that I never knew could consume me this much. I was such a worldly gal. And by "worldly," I mean, living in the world, not the spirit, or as I like to say, for my Jesus. So this was a change. I liked to make jokes with lots of curses. I liked sin. Not the hurting other people kind of sin. Just the make me happy kind. Whatever that was.

And just like that, it was gone. The desire to sin or do things that would hurt my relationship with Jesus—gone. Didn't bother me one bit either. Thank you, Jesus. I wasn't aware that I was hurting myself. I was hindering my ability to receive the gifts that Jesus died to give me. Yup. He set me up. What next?

CHAPTER
2

HOLY SPIRIT POWER–YES, PLEASE

When you are born again, that very instant, you are guaranteed a place in heaven. Your spirit is now as perfect as Jesus. What could be better? I couldn't think of anything. But, while we're here on earth, we are to be blessed with all the promises, gifts, and protection from God. One of the promises Jesus gave us was the Holy Spirit He would leave with us when He went to heaven. The baptism of the Holy Spirit.

The night before Jesus was crucified, He explained in John 16:7, "Nevertheless I tell you the truth; It is expedient for you that I go away: for if I go not away, the Comforter will not come unto you; but if I depart, I will send him unto you."

The Holy Spirit is the power of the Holy Trinity: God the Father, God the Son, God the Holy Spirit. When God conceives, even from the beginning of time, the Holy Spirit moves into action. He is the power that performs what God conceives and Jesus spoke.

When I received prayer to accept the Holy Spirit, it was like an amplification of all my desire to learn, and a mighty warrior rose up inside. I now had the ability to pray in tongues, controversial as it may be. A power and force given to us which enhances our ability to hear, know, and receive from the Lord. Thank you, Jesus. You want this. Dig in and research and learn about it. Study. Receive it. Pray for it.

Jesus didn't even start His own ministry until He received

the power of the Holy Spirit. And neither should we. Zechariah 4:6 tells us, "'Not by might nor by power, but by my Spirit,' says the LORD Almighty."

Galatians 5:22–23 explains: "But the fruit of the Spirit is love, joy, peace, longsuffering, gentleness, goodness, faith, meekness, temperance: against such there is no law." I will gladly live a life with these fruits working from within me. Submission and acceptance of the Holy Spirit will help produce these fruits in your life, and so much more.

These gifts from our Lord are the beginning of knowing who you are. WHO you are in Christ. What you mean to Him. God loves us so much He sent His Son to die for us. To be the ransom for our sin. Prior to that, we had no way to go directly to God. He made it so.

What else does He say about us? What else is there in a relationship with Jesus that makes me who I am, helps me, comforts me, provides for me, protects me? Why would I want any of this?

CHAPTER

3

WHAT DOES GOD SAY ABOUT ME?

Did you know that, once born again, you are ROYALTY? Right on! "But you are a chosen race, a royal priesthood, a holy nation, a people for his own possession" (1 Peter 2:9). "For he is Lord of lords and King of kings, and those with him are called and chosen and faithful" (Revelation 17: 14).

Prior to knowing Christ, I never would have walked around with the belief that I was even close to that category, let alone "royalty." It was not in my structure to be full of myself. In fact, my self-esteem was pretty low. Life beat me pretty hard for a long time. I had determination, but not much confidence. And here comes Jesus. To tell me all about myself and what He thinks of His creation! Wow! It's revelation knowledge. Say it out loud. Speak it out over yourself every day. Let it simmer. I - AM - ROYALTY. The words you speak have power. Power to bless or to curse the life you are living right now. Speak out what the Lord says about you!

And here we have one of the reasons I can think and believe what He says about me: "Therefore, if anyone is in Christ, he is a new creation. The old has passed away; behold, the new has come" (2 Corinthians 5:17). The new...thoughtfully and carefully accept that you are NEW. "I have been crucified with Christ. It is no longer I who live, but Christ who lives in me. And the life I now live in the flesh I live by faith in the Son of God, who loved me and gave himself for me" (Galatians 2:20). Believe and receive. Receive EVERYTHING the Lord has to give and say about you and for you.

Trusting, believing, and receiving God's Word is an absolute necessity as we walk in the world of today. Especially what He says about us. Without it, we tend to believe what the world says. We become oppressed, depressed, weak, despondent, frail, and filled with anxiety and fear. Knowing what God says about you—walking in the truth, living it—will change your life walk. Hope, joy, love, strength, and peace will all replace the world view. Thank you, Jesus. Even though we have difficulties, we know we are not alone. We will persevere with new strength and come out better because of our new identity.

I am created in God's own image (Genesis 1:27); chosen and holy (1 Peter 2:9); sanctified (Jeremiah 1:5); a member of the body of Christ (1 Corinthians 12:27); a friend of God (John 15:15); purified (1 John 3:1–3); the temple of the Holy Ghost (1 Corinthians 6:19–20); an heir with Christ (Galatians 3:27–29); a believer with power (John 1:12); strong (2 Timothy 1:7); blessed (Ephesians 1:3); and free (Romans 8:2–30 John 8:31–32). Oh, but there's more...so much more!

Get this down into your soul. These words are power. Know them. Live them. From your spirit, to your soul, into your body.

CHAPTER
4

EXPOUNDING ON THE POWER

Walking in the knowledge of what the Lord says about you is freeing. It lifts you to a point of confidence you weren't aware was a reality. And it makes you realize that everything you thought was important—work, bills, status, material possessions, and the like—were not the drive behind your existence. it's been God all along. He has been the force, the push, the life force in your every move. Now it's all coming together.

Knowledge is power in more than one way. Knowing what God says about you is empowering and pushes you further into His will for you. And continuing in that knowledge is life.

My son, do not forget my teaching, but let your heart keep my commandments, for length of days and years of life and peace they will add to you. Let not steadfast love and faithfulness forsake you; bind them around your neck; write them on the tablet of your heart. So you will find favor and good success in the sight of God and man. Trust in the Lord with all your heart, and do not lean on your own understanding.

Proverbs 3:1–35

That very power, that knowledge, is like a medicine. You learn, you absorb, you know, you live it, you heal. It's a medicine that is life altering. And you collect knowledge and insight. The Holy Spirit works from within you. Leading, guiding, sharing.

Not so long after I started living for Christ, my son experienced a demonic oppression. Something I would have chalked up to hormones or moodiness and change before knowing what I know now. By united prayer and anointing with the power given to us by Jesus, he was set free. In an instant, mind you, after months of torment. "And these signs shall follow them that believe; In my name shall they cast out devils; they shall speak with new tongues; They shall take up serpents; and if they drink any deadly thing, it shall not hurt them; they shall lay hands on the sick, and they shall recover" (Mark 16:17–18, KJV). Thank you, Jesus.

This isn't to say you will ever need to remove demons or stop an oppressive spirit. And believe me when I say they are out there. But when you know WHO you are in Christ, you will walk and pull from that power within you every day. Those worldly things that come across your path, those whispers that say you are not good enough, that fear that keeps you from moving forward in life, those things that are not from God— they will be squashed with that power. Knowing the authority and power Christ suffered to give us is a whole new level of life. I want that for you. Jesus wants that for you.

CHAPTER
5

HIS LOVE = NOTHING IN THIS WORLD COMPARES

Have you ever had that feeling from inside that something wasn't quite right? My mother used to say it was my woman's intuition. Standing in a room full of people and listening to conversation and knowing something was "off" about that person speaking. Or walk into a room and the hairs on the back of your neck stand up. Or your child is not with you, but you can just feel that something has happened and you need to get to them. I had that. My whole life. And it wasn't intuition, clairvoyance, insight, or the like. It was the Holy Spirit. It was a gift from God through the Holy Spirit that I hadn't tuned into yet. Remember those gifts that were listed before?

I was sitting at a red light in the left turn lane one day years ago. The road I was turning on went up over the interstate. As the light turned to signal for me to go, something said *don't move*. It was not an audible voice. It came from deep inside. One, two, three seconds passed. From the left, a car came racing through the intersection at an extremely high speed. So high, in fact, I don't remember the vehicle. Only the FACT that if I would have pulled forward to make my turn, that car would have crashed into my door and, most likely, killed me instantly.

We do not know what the Lord is up to. We don't know His plan. But even then, as I was living my life for me and NOT for God, He was watching over, protecting, and directing me. What else has he done that we are not aware of? I can assure you the list is endless.

Now that I know Him, now that I have a relationship with the Lord, I see why He did what He did for me. Why He continues to do for me. Nobody, and I mean nobody, will ever love me like that. I am His creation.

> For we are his workmanship, created in Christ Jesus for good works, which God prepared beforehand, that we should walk in them.
>
> Ephesians 2:10
>
> For I am sure that neither death nor life, nor angels nor rulers, nor things present nor things to come, nor powers, nor height nor depth, nor anything else in all creation, will be able to separate us from the love of God in Christ Jesus our Lord.
>
> Romans 8:38–39 (NIV)

I mean, are you hearing that? Really let that sink in. Recite it out loud for all your senses to absorb. I am praying for you right now to receive that love from the Lord. Feel it wash over you and sink deep inside you.

Now, carry that with you wherever you go. In everything you do. KNOW it. You are a masterpiece. You are loved beyond what love could ever be on this earth. WHO you are in Christ is fueled by that love every second of every day. Live it.

CHAPTER

LABOR-FREE WAGES

That is the truth. I'm really not kidding. The gifts from God are labor free. We are covered by His grace thanks to the work Jesus completed at the Cross. This is another piece to the puzzle of learning WHO you are in Christ.

There is nothing we have to work for to complete or earn His gifts. You don't have to be perfect, act perfect, never make a mistake, pray harder to win Him over, or whatever else. It's true. There is nothing, outside your belief and confession of faith, that you need to do. And there is nothing, absolutely NOTHING, that He will not forgive. Jesus loves you as you are.

I didn't know that. I would tell myself, "as soon as I quit this bad habit and straighten up, I'll go to church." I believed that was what was needed for me to be presentable enough to be accepted by God. As if I had to clean myself up first. WRONG.

To try or to put work forth in order to "please" or "win" Him over would be the same as telling Jesus His suffering and death on the Cross wasn't good enough. "Let me add in some extra special prayers to get an answer from God sooner." No. Absolutely not the correct approach.

It's done. There's nothing you can do or say to change or improve what Christ has done for us. It is finished. Jesus said so on the Cross. At that point, we went from law to grace. There was no turning back.

Jesus didn't seek out the "perfect" or those who were

without blemish. He walked with sinners and tax collectors and thieves. "Jesus answered them, 'It is not the healthy who need a doctor, but the sick. I have not come to call the righteous, but sinners to repentance'" (Luke 5:31–32, NIV).

That is not to say that we shouldn't work toward our goals, work for a living, earn a wage, and so on. The Bible tells us in Deuteronomy 28:12 (NIV) "The Lord will open the heavens, the storehouses of his bounty, to send rain on your land in season and to *bless all the work of your hands."* The promises are numerous. They are yours for the taking. You need only to believe and receive.

> For you know the grace of our Lord Jesus Christ, that though he was rich, yet for your sake he became poor, so that you through his poverty might become rich.
>
> 2 Corinthians 8:9 (NIV)
>
> For the LORD delights in his people; he crowns the humble with victory.
>
> Psalm 149:4 (NLT)
>
> Take delight in the Lord, and he will give you the desires of your heart.
>
> Psalm 37:4 (NIV)

And they overcame him by the blood of the Lamb, and by the word of their testimony.

Revelations 12:11

And all thy children shall be taught of the Lord; and great shall be the peace of thy children.

Isaiah 54:13

I let the peace of God rule in my heart and I refuse to worry about anything.

Colossians 3:15

In righteousness shall you be established: you shall be far from oppression; for you shall not fear: and from terror; for it shall not come near you.

Isaiah 54:14

For he will command his angels concerning you to guard you in all your ways.

Psalm 91:11

There's more. Study the Word of God and know these promises. Know WHO you are, what you are entitled to as a child of God, what power you have, and more!

CHAPTER
7

THESE, THOU, WHO, WHAT?

My first venture into reading the Bible was interesting. I had a copy of the King James Version given to me. It was a paperback novel version, and I sat down with it like I was going to read a good book. I anticipated some great knowledge, and I knew I would read through it and know so much by the time I was finished.

It was a great thought. That's just not how it happened. Here I am a decade or so into my love of Christ and still, I have yet to read the entire Bible. That is not to say that I haven't studied the books and reviewed or touched on stories from all or most of the books but, it is an adventure that will go on throughout my life. My faith brings me to it. I absolutely need to be in the Word of God. "So then faith *comes* by hearing, and hearing by the word of God" (Romans 10:17, NKJV).

This is not a book to read cover to cover, beginning to end. This is God's living, breathing Word of truth and life. It is our instruction manual for how to live, what to do and not to do. This is the Divinely Authorized Word of God. What does that mean? It means that God spoke through the authors. If there are different versions, and there are, it is because there were teams of scholars, doctors of divinity, truly holy people who worked through the Holy Spirit to rewrite the original words. Trust in it. Know it.

God is not a man, that he should lie; neither the son of man, that he should repent: hath he said, and shall he not do it? or hath he spoken, and shall he not make it good?

Numbers 23:19 (KJV)

Whoever is of God hears the words of God. The reason why you do not hear them is that you are not of God.

John 8:47

And your ears shall hear a word behind you, saying, "This is the way, walk in it," when you turn to the right or when you turn to the left.

Isaiah 30:21 (NIV)

It is the Spirit who gives life; the flesh is no help at all.

John 6:63

All Scripture is breathed out by God and profitable for teaching, for reproof, for correction, and for training in righteousness.

2 Timothy 3:16 (NIV)

Lesson upon lesson. Values, morals, principles. Everything that you will go through in life has an example or instruction in the Bible. Discipline, Love, work, health, wealth, immortality, obedience, morality, vengeance, tenacity, honor—even witchcraft and sorcery—on and on it goes.

Really consider this truthfully. How many movies have been made from the stories in the Bible? Where else can you learn so much and receive so much? It's all compacted into the books of the Bible. It has the story of Creation, our Creator, our Savior, and every character in between. There is meaning and life in every word. It really does live and breathe.

The most read book in the world is the Christian Bible. In the fifty years preceding 2012, there were 3.9 billion copies sold, which is a very interesting fact. It has stood the test of time. Amazing.

There are several versions. You can research them all, but the one I started with is the Amplified Bible, which captures the full meaning of the Greek and Hebrew versions. There are foundations who work hundreds of thousands of hours preparing text to be true to the original versions and to ensure to give Jesus his proper place in their versions. The Amplified gives a breakdown and further explanation of the writings. For example, "But these are written (recorded) in order that you may believe that Jesus is the Christ (the Anointed One) the Son of God" (John 20:31).

There are study Bibles, breakdowns of books of the Bible, and apps where you can read and change the various versions to enhance the full meaning of the verse. It's wonderful how easy it is to review the Word and receive messages from the Lord.

As for a plan, you can research online to find the best study plan. I started with the Gospels (the good news) of Matthew, Mark, Luke, and John. The stories are told from different perspectives of Jesus' walk on earth.

The best direction I can give is to make sure you are in a good Bible-based church and you use the Bible as your instruction manual for life. Never stop learning from it. Share it. Reference it with every question you have in life. Look at all the versions and really know what it says about and for you. It holds ALL our answers. It is the Living Word of God.

CHAPTER

8

PRAY LIKE YOU KNOW HIM

I used to think that in order to pray to God, I had to have some long, drawn-out pretentious style poem with words that I barely understood and a lot of "thees" and "thous." Wrong. Not the truth at all. Now I pray based on everything I know about Jesus and what He did for us all. That is not to say that the eloquent prayers that are out there aren't effectual. But you do need to know that you can go to Him as you are. James 4:8 says: "Draw near to God and He will draw near to you." Isaiah 1:18, "Come now, let us reason together, says the Lord: though your sins are like scarlet, they shall be as white as snow; though they are red like crimson, they shall become like wool."

Jesus taught us how to pray here:

> And when you pray, do not be like the hypocrites, for they love to pray standing in the synagogues and on the street corners to be seen by others. Truly I tell you, they have received their reward in full. But when you pray, go into your room, close the door and pray to your Father, who is unseen. Then your Father, who sees what is done in secret, will reward you. And when you pray, do not keep on babbling like pagans, for they think they will be heard because of their many words. Do not be like them, for your Father knows what you need before you ask him.
>
> Matthew 6: 5–8 5 (NIV)

I talk to Jesus every day. When I wake up, I wish Him a good morning. When I go to bed, I thank Him for everything He has done for me. When I have questions or need help with things, I talk to Him. When something happens, I want to talk to Him. That is prayer. I build my relationship with Him every day. Sometimes not as much as others. Some days, not at all. But that is because my own focus is off. Because I let the world lead me instead of Him.

I was taught that when I have a specific need, or when I am praying for the need of another to follow these simple steps:

1. Request the need to the Lord.

2. Find the scripture that backs/meets the need.

3. Meditate on it-speak out ONLY what the Word of God says about it.

4. Believe in my heart and mind that it is done...as if I have already received it.

5. Thank Him that I have received it.

6. Give Him all the praise and glory for handing it over to me.

It really is that simple (and man, is it powerful!). Prayer is talking, building your relationship, keeping in touch regularly with the Lord. Here is a good example of making a request in prayer: *Lord, I know Your Word says that You will bless the work of my hands, so I am asking for that promotion to come through at work! I thank you for it, Lord, and I give You all the glory!* But talking to Him about your daily things and what is going on is prayer as well.

Did you know that when you pray according to His Word, the angels hearken to your prayer? In Daniel 9:21 an angel came to Daniel and said, "The moment you began praying, a command was given. And now I am here to tell you what it was, for you are very precious to God." When you speak the Word of God and stand on it in your prayer, the angels get to work. When you speak things contrary to the Word of God, the angels can't carry it out. Things like*: It'll never work out; I'm never getting that new job; I am sick as a dog;* and so on. Our words must be in line with what He says about it.

Prayer is one of THE most powerful weapons we have against the enemy. Don't ever forget that.

CHAPTER
9

SPEAK WISELY

My whole life, the things that came out of my mouth were not of much concern to me. I say that not to be flippant. I was never cross to people who didn't cross me or rude or hurtful to others. What is meant here is that I just rolled along with it all. When life kicked me down, I spoke it out. I cried out, *Why is my life in such a ruin? What did I do to deserve this?* When life was good, I spoke out things like, *Man, sometimes I'm not the sharpest tool in the shed—ha ha. This job is going to be the death of me.* Looking in the mirror, I'd say, *You are fat.* I spoke over my body: *My feet are killing me. This pain is never going to go away.* Boy, if I knew then what I know now.

The Bible tells us in Proverbs 18:21:

> Death and life are in the power of the tongue, and those who love it will eat its fruits.

As well as Ephesians 4:29:

> Let no corrupting talk come out of your mouths, but only such as is good for building up, as fits the occasion, that it may give grace to those who hear.

And Proverbs 12:18:

> There is one whose rash words are like sword thrusts, but the tongue of the wise brings healing."
> Our words have power. We must be mindful of everything we speak.

God spoke our world into existence. He spoke in Genesis 1:3:

> And God said, Let there be light: and there was light.

And God spoke again in Genesis 1:6:

> And God said, Let there be a firmament in the midst of the waters, and let it divide the waters from the waters.

And God spoke again in Genesis 1:9:

> And God said, Let the waters under the heaven be gathered together unto one place, and let the dry land appear: and it was so. He spoke our world, all of creation, into existence.

The power of creation in the spoken word is magnificent.

Remember when we talked about prayer? How meditating and speaking out the Word that backs your need or request was important? It is because you are speaking life. The Word of God is life and truth. Speaking it out fills your atmosphere with the Holy Word and hearkens those angels to move. Speaking against the Word, or truth, does the opposite. It is real. It is necessary on a constant basis to be aware of every word we speak. Choose: Life-building words or death.

Think about it. Do you want your child to grow into a wise, productive, God-fearing man or woman, or do you want them to be a debt to society—not moving ahead in life, always struggling, fearful, and weak? What do you say about your children every day? Do you lift them up? *You are so smart and fun. You are going places in life, child! I know you can do it!* Or are you speaking the opposite? *Why do you have to be such a pain?* You are planting the seeds, through the spirit, that will mature and grow into what you say it will. Believe it. Know it to be true.

Again, consider this carefully. You become a born-again believer in Christ by "CONFESSING with your mouth" (Romans 10:9). Because, if you confess with your mouth that Jesus is Lord and believe in your heart that God raised him from the dead, you will be saved." It is a very real principle in the world right now.

It works to the contrary as well. Why do you think witches cast spells? They speak them out with their wicked tongues and plant the seed for the evil to take route. It's not a game. It is real. Evil is real. The spirit world is real. You have to make yourself conscious of the power of your tongue.

There was a fantastic evangelist who wrote a series of small booklets about God's creative power. He taught me that when you speak out life it changes your course. It moves you in the direction you are meant to go. And believe me when I say it has dramatically changed my life for the better. Thank you, Lord!

Remember this. Study the Word and know what it says about how your words plant those seeds. Don't give the enemy a foothold in your life to come in and wreak havoc over you or your loved ones.

> For the word of God is living and active, sharper than any two-edged sword, piercing to the division of soul and of spirit, of joints and of marrow, and discerning the thoughts and intentions of the heart.
>
> Hebrews 4:12
>
> Whoever guards his mouth preserves his life; he who opens wide his lips comes to ruin.
>
> Proverbs 13:3

Don't be "Hung by your Tongue."

CHAPTER
10

THE OPPOSITION

Speaking of the enemy, I mean to tell you that I am not giving him any glory here. And I vow to make this the shortest chapter in this book because he doesn't deserve any of our attention. But he is real.

The enemy is good for smokescreens and lies. He's all smoke and mirrors and he has no new tricks up his sleeve. But here's what you need to know. You have the ultimate power to overcome him and his schemes. Woooohoooo! Know it!

When Jesus died on the Cross, He stole the keys to hell and left that enemy out to dry. We know the end of the story—he loses. And we, by Jesus' work at the Cross, have been given the keys and power:

Behold, I give unto you power to tread on serpents and scorpions, and over all the power of the enemy: and nothing shall by any means hurt you.

Luke 10:19 (KJV)

And these signs will follow those who believe: In My name they will cast out demons; they will speak with new tongues; they will take up serpents; and if they drink anything deadly, it will by no means hurt them; they will lay hands on the sick, and they will recover.

Mark 16:17–18 (NKJV)

This is another key and revelational truth to knowing WHO you are in Christ.

He is a liar, and the Word tells us in John 10:10, "The thief comes only to steal and kill and destroy; I have come that they may have life, and have it to the full." The most important part of this scripture is that Jesus came to give us life.

Know that, as a born-again believer, you are above the enemy. You do not need to fall for his schemes. Everything that is thrown against you (doubt, fear, hate, anger, haughtiness, lust, and so on) is not from God. Keep your focus on the things of God and don't glorify or give any focus to the enemy. He will poke and prod you but, when you know who you are, you have a world overcoming power on the inside of you that can overcome anything.

The best defense is a great offense. When the enemy throws his darts—like the memories of the person or persons who hurt me, or how it didn't work out, or when I didn't have that prayer answered—I have vowed to myself that I will pray harder over that situation. I will pray for those who hurt me. Out loud I will let the enemy and his minions know that they poked me right into praying for the someone they used to push me and get me off track. I can be crafty too. And I love my Jesus way too much to let a chump push me into hurting my relationship with Him. It's not always 100 percent, but most times it is good. Matthew 5:44 (NIV) "But I say, love your enemies! Pray for those who persecute you!" Hard as it may be at times, it is right.

CHAPTER
11

GO WITH THE PEACE

Every day I learn something new about the Lord and His kingdom. It's my joy. It's what I look forward to. I have learned from so many pastors and leaders over the years, but my best friend and mentor, Cris, was the one who taught me the foundations. She gave me knowledge—untainted, faith-filled knowledge. She filled my heart and my mind with the truths of how the kingdom works. She prayed for and with me. We were quite a pair. She also gave me the best advice I have ever received. She told me that when you are faced with a hard choice to go with the peace. I wasn't quite sure what she meant at first. I mean, I did, but I didn't know it like I know it now.

Have you ever had a choice to make, and you weren't quite sure which way to go with it? They both seem to be a good idea, but you can't get to the point of choosing? Go with the peace. If you have prayed on it, considered the options, looked at all angles, and you still don't feel peace, then don't do it. It is sound advice. The Holy Spirit will guide you. "But when he, the Spirit of truth, comes, he will guide you into all the truth. He will not speak on his own; he will speak only what he hears, and he will tell you what is yet to come" John 16:13.

Knowing what God says about me has changed everything. Before, I would shake the eight ball or hope for the best, not knowing if I was walking into disaster or victory. I didn't pray about anything or ask God for advice. As I said before, I was a worldly gal. I would ask my friends or my family what they thought I should do. Some things worked out, some didn't. But now, I know that peace. I can enter into a change, agreement, contract, whatever knowing that God has opened that door. It's not 100 percent. I'm not a prophet, and I don't have a direct line to the answers. What I do have, though, is a complete trust in what God says in His word and the gift that Jesus sent to us when He left: the Holy Spirit.

CHAPTER
12

MIRACLES ARE FOR NOW

The days of Jesus' walk on earth were miraculous. Reading through the gospels fills you with the wondrous power and works He did while he was with us on earth. But it wasn't just for that time. Miracles are for now. Did you know that the Word says in John 14:12 (NRSV), "Verily, verily, I say unto you, He that believeth on me, the works that I do shall he do also; and greater works than these shall he do; because I go unto the Father." Ya. Get excited!

My husband had an injury to a tendon just below his thumb joint, and it never healed the way it should have. He could barely move his thumb. The specialist found that the tendon wasn't repaired correctly, and that it was shriveling up and not in use. The day of his surgery to attempt repair, I asked the doctor, "What is the best-case scenario?" He stated, "The best case would have been that we open him up and that tendon is right there to repair, but that is off the table now as the MRI showed the tendon has shrunk up, and we need to graft one from elsewhere." So I replied, "Well, I'm believing for the best-case scenario. I know how my God works."

The doctor smiled kindly and stated it would be about 2–3 hours for the surgery. About 35–40 minutes into the wait, the doctor came through the waiting room doors yelling my name, "Gibson! Gibson!" I stood up as the room was packed with other day surgery family and friends waiting on their patients. The doctor ran to me and said, "He's all done!" I said, kind of sarcastically, "But you said 2–3 hours." He said, very enthusi-astically, "There's no scientific reason for it, but that tendon was sitting right there and it is repaired!" I said, "I'm not an 'I told you so' kind of gal, but...." That doctor knew without a doubt it was God. He cares about everything we go through. And belief brought that miracle into the natural. Thank you, Lord!

One day while on the road for work, I was coming around a right curve into one of the local small towns. At the end of the curve in the opposite lane is a turn lane to cross onto one of the busy crossroads, but I have the right of way at a speed of 45 mph. The car that was in that turn lane while I was coming around the curve misjudged and turned just feet in front of me. I braced for impact, as there was no time to stop. I could see the whites of the driver's eyes. All of a sudden, my car moved sideways as if ten linebackers hit me on the passenger side of the car and pushed it directly west. I felt my body shift to the right with the jolt. I looked, and that car was moving past me into the turn and on their way they went. I've never felt anything like that in all the years of driving automobiles. The only expla-nation was divine intervention. All of my work papers, purse, drink, and loose items were spewed throughout the front cabin. I was in awe of the whole incident. It was a miracle. Thank you, Lord!

In my years of living for myself, I was a smoker. It was a habit I enjoyed and never had the desire to quit. Well, things change, and just as with all the desires I had prior to really knowing Him, He removed this was one I wanted gone. Although, I really didn't want to let go. I wanted to keep this one. I had a fear of what would happen if I quit. It had been so many years, and this was a crutch I relied on. So, with that being said, I allowed the enemy to dig those claws in fully. Well, I had just had it. I was done. I prayed for the Lord to take that desire away, and my heart was ready. But I felt I needed some assistance. My pastor made an altar call. Anyone with requests could come up and she would pray for you. I was fully determined to dump this demonic addiction. And so I whispered to Pastor my need. She didn't even fully raise her hands to pray over me when I felt as if a surge of electricity was pushing me back and out I went. Down to the floor, for I don't know how long. When I woke, I was free. The Lord removed the desire after over thirty years of addiction. Thank you, Lord!

Our youngest son worked in roofing and gutters. One day I received a call that he had fallen two stories onto concrete and was on his way to the hospital via ambulance. Mind you, I pray daily. I speak life and protection over my bloodline and cover them all in the armor of God every day. I had an hour's drive to get to him. I felt the fear pushing up against me. I rebuked it. I prayed in the Spirit as I drove, and I thanked God that our son was fine and had minor injuries, if any. I called our pastor to meet us at the hospital. I thanked God like I've never thanked Him before. I thanked Him that He gives His angels charge over us (Psalm 91). I thanked Him that with long life He will satisfy us. I thanked Him that all was well with our child.

Upon arrival, no answers were given. They wouldn't let us in the ER. I kept praying until they allowed us in and the doctor explained that "he was a very lucky boy." He fell through an unstable roof, two stories, and caught his pants and boot on the ladder, which slowed the velocity of the fall. He had a broken pinky and a twisted knee. He did hit his head and may have had a slight concussion as well. The first words out of our pastor's mouth were, "Thank God for praying mothers!" Thank you, Lord! Luck was not a factor. God was!

A few decades ago, my pastor was picking up his dinner at one of the locally owned bar and grills. While he was waiting, a man sitting at the bar fell backward off his stool and laid on the floor, lifeless. Pastor Robert ran to him, as someone who knows about first aid and assisting in situations like this. He stated that as he bent down over the man to check his breathing and pulse, he knew instantly that he had died. There were very evident signs, including losing control of all bodily functions. Pastor Robert checked, and the man had no pulse and was not breathing. He was lifeless. Pastor Robert then prepared to start chest compressions immediately and administer CPR and was positioned over the man's body. As he did, he said this feeling of electricity started in his shoulders and traveled down both arms and as he cupped his hands to begin, he felt the powerful surge leave his arms. He hadn't even touched the man when suddenly the man's head popped up and he spoke. He actually stood up, embarrassed, and had to run to the restroom.

Just a very few weeks ago, during the work of writing this very book, my granddaughter was hit by a car. She is twelve years old and has an extremely gentle and loving spirit.

That very morning, while finishing my morning prayer and readings, I got up and started off to work. I very distinctly heard the Holy Spirit tell me that I hadn't put on the armor.

Every day, I pray and "loose" or speak out over all my bloodline—my family and those I pray for—the armor of God.

Put on the whole armour of God, that ye may be able to stand against the wiles of the devil. For we wrestle not against flesh and blood, but against principalities, against powers, against the rulers of the darkness of this world, against spiritual wickedness in high places. Wherefore take unto you the whole armour of God, that ye may be able to withstand in the evil day, and having done all, to stand. Stand therefore, having your loins girt about with truth, and having on the breastplate of righteousness; And your feet shod with the preparation of the gospel of peace; Above all, taking the shield of faith, wherewith ye shall be able to quench all the fiery darts of the wicked. And take the helmet of salvation, and the sword of the Spirit, which is the word of God: Praying always

45

> with all prayer and supplication in the Spirit, and watching thereunto with all perseverance and supplication for all saints.
>
> Ephesians 6:11–18 (KJV)

My two granddaughters had run back into the large shopping center to grab something that was forgotten when shopping with their mom. As they were heading back out, my 12-year-old granddaughter ran out first and a smaller van had stopped for her. A car behind them went around the van and hit her as she was running across the drive. The car knocked her down and ran over her leg. She was injured from the knee down. It broke her leg in several places. Horrific as it was, I believe it could have been extremely worse. The fact that only one leg was injured and there were no other injuries after being struck then run over, to me, is miraculous. Thank God for His protection. It is very real.

There are testimonies upon testimonies of miracles daily. Your belief has EVERYTHING to do with receiving what the Lord has for you. Miracles, yes. But blessing even more! I want to walk in the blessings and promises daily! As I know you do. Keep learning, keep growing, keep on the knowledge and believe what He says.

> But if God so clothes the grass of the field, which is alive today and tomorrow is thrown into the furnace, will He not much more clothe you? You of little faith! Do not worry then, saying, "What will we eat?'" or "What will we drink?" or "What will we wear for clothing?" For the Gentiles eagerly seek all these things; for your heavenly Father knows that you need all these things. But seek first His kingdom and His righteousness, and all these things will be added to you.
>
> Matthew 6:30–33

In Daniel 11:32, "He will flatter and win over those who have violated the covenant. *But the people who know their God* will be strong and will resist him." He's talking about knowing God, knowing Him through the Word. It is power. Power to resist the temptation and lies of the enemy, but power in knowing that what God says is true. That belief is the bridge that manifests the miracles and blessings into the natural world from the spiritual.

CHAPTER
13

BE RESPONSIBLE

As you gain knowledge in studying the Word of God, you are responsible for it. "Do your best to present yourself to God as one approved, a worker who does not need to be ashamed and who correctly handles the word of truth (2 Timothy 2:15, NIV). As you learn your wants and needs should be changing and your life will revolve around what the word says and how He wants you to live.

This is a longer, but really great, example of how we should follow the Word in treating others:

In reply Jesus said: "A man was going down from Jerusalem to Jericho, when he was attacked by robbers. They stripped him of his clothes, beat him and went away, leaving him half dead. A priest happened to be going down the same road, and when he saw the man, he passed by on the other side. So too, a Levite, when he came to the place and saw him, passed by on the other side. But a Samaritan, as he traveled, came where the man was; and when he saw him, he took pity on him. He went to him and bandaged his wounds, pouring on oil and wine. Then he put the man on his own donkey, brought him to an inn and took care of him. The next day he took out two denarii and gave them to the innkeeper. 'Look after him,' he said, 'and when I return, I will

> reimburse you for any extra expense you may have.'
> "Which of these three do you think was a neighbor
> to the man who fell into the hands of robbers?" The
> expert in the law replied, "The one who had mercy
> on him." Jesus told him, "Go and do likewise."
>
> Luke 10:30–37 (NIV)

This is a verse that tells us how we should treat our family: "Who does not provide for their relatives, and especially for their own household, has denied the faith and is worse than an unbeliever" (1 Timothy 5:8, NIV).

Here is a verse that tells us how to handle money: "Keep your lives free from the love of money and be content with what you have, because God has said, 'Never will I leave you; never will I forsake you'" (Hebrews 13:5).

The point here is that when we have to make an account for all of our actions, God will know what you have done and if you were true to Him. When you learn His ways, you must follow. He will know your heart in all things you do and have done. Be responsible for what you have learned. Apply it to your life all day, every day. When you live for the Lord and love Him, it is much easier to live by His Word and commandments. It is something you will want to do without hesitation.

CHAPTER
14

DON'T BEND THE TRUTH

As you learn, you are not only responsible for that godly knowledge, but you should not change or alter the Word to fit your own personal needs. The truth is law. It is laid out for us in such a way that we should never add or take away from what is being said. "Ye shall not add unto the word which I command you, neither shall ye diminish ought from it, that ye may keep the commandments of the LORD your God which I command you" (Deuteronomy 4:2, KJV).

That is not to say you shouldn't study all the available versions. Studying that way can help you to understand the true meaning or what God is saying to you at that moment and time.

Studying a certain topic in various versions of the Bible will help you to gain meaning, but I always suggest you look at more than one scripture to expand the meaning. For example, study what God says about pride:

God opposes the proud but gives grace to the humble.

James 4:6

Toward the scorners he is scornful, but to the humble he gives favor.

Proverbs 3:34

> I say to the boastful, "Do not boast," and to the
> wicked, "Do not lift up your horn."
>
> Psalm 75:4

So we can deduce that God opposes pride and learn even more by continuing to learn what He says about it by searching out additional scripture. You can use your Bible concordance to find additional scripture or do an online search.

We want to make sure that we grasp the full meaning and we don't waiver from what the Lord says. Remember that the Word is truth. We need to have a reverence and complete respect for it and live to the best of our ability conforming to God's Word.

> All scripture is given by inspiration of God, and is
> profitable for doctrine, for reproof, for correction, for
> instruction in righteousness.
>
> 2 Timothy 3:16
>
> Knowing this first, that no prophecy of the scripture
> is of any private interpretation.
>
> 2 Peter 1:20

And you will know the truth, and the truth will set you free."

John 8:32

Stand therefore, having fastened on the belt of truth, and having put on the breastplate of righteousness.

Ephesians 6:14

Our focus on the absolute truth will keep us in line with God's plan for us. Praying in line with His truth will feed us knowledge and standing on His promises will bless us. "The Lord is near to all who call on him, to all who call on him in truth" (Psalm 145:18). If we don't have a full understanding or we twist what God says to make it fit our own agenda, then we fall short. "When you ask, you do not receive, because you ask with wrong motives, that you may spend what you get on your pleasures" (James 4:3, NIV). Always pray for the Holy Spirit to guide you in your studies to ensure you are on the right track.

CHAPTER
15

WHY IS THE WORLD SUCH A MESS?

The world has a HUGE misconception of who God is and of who causes the problems the world faces today, including death. Why do bad things happen? The world is also very blind to the fact that there is a spiritual world that contains good and evil. And that we have a choice of who we will serve.

Remember John 10:10? "The thief comes only to steal and kill and destroy; I have come that they may have life, and have it to the full." This is a quick breakdown and truth that explains, in a nutshell, who is in charge of what in the spiritual world.

Have you ever walked through one of those tunnel aquariums? It is a wonderful, beautiful experience. Especially if the aquarium is packed full of colorful marine life. My husband and I were blessed with this experience on a trip to Dallas some years back. Now, imagine yourself reaching up into that aquarium and grabbing at some of that beauty as if that glass were like a membrane. That's a cool visual. And it is very similar to the spiritual world, except we walk surrounded, wherever we go with the spiritual world. It is there whether you believe or don't believe in it.

A few years ago, I was praying and spending time with the Lord. He gave me a vision similar to the reaching into the aquarium visual we just went over. Except I was on a ladder and when I reached the ceiling, I realized it wasn't a ceiling at all but more of a membrane-type material. I used my hands to spread it open as if I was opening curtains and popped the top of my head through and I was able to see some of the floor of what I believe was heaven. It was colorful and busy. I only saw movement from an ant's perspective. It was a blur but an amazing experience. I felt like someone was pouring out love from a bucket all over me (remember that love I explained before). There is nothing this world or the people in it can give us.

During the time my son was experiencing demonic oppression, I had experiences as well that were tied to his situation. In prayer one day, with my eyes closed, the devil came to my face. I actually felt and smelled hot stinky breath and saw his horrible and disgusting face in mine. I felt the tangible presence of his hate for me. It was startling, to say the least. But it was revelatory to me as well. He is real. And he hates us all, especially we who love the Lord and work to save people from the devil's clutches. I have to say, I know now that this particular experience told me that I was on the right path. Why else would he try to scare me? It didn't work, by the way. I am stronger and fight even harder now. I am a warrior of God!

I share these experiences to, again, let you know that it is all real but also to explain that the bad things that happen in the world are not from God. Evil breeds evil and bad things happen. Sin allows evil into your life.

Now the works of the flesh are evident: sexual immorality, impurity, sensuality, idolatry, sorcery,

> enmity, strife, jealousy, fits of anger, rivalries,
> dissensions, divisions, envy, drunkenness, orgies,
> and things like these. I warn you, as I warned you
> before, that those who do such things will not inherit
> the kingdom of God.
>
> Galatians 5:19–21
>
> For the wages of sin is death, but the free gift of God
> is eternal life in Christ Jesus our Lord.
>
> Romans 6:23

Sin = Death. Whether spiritual or physical death. Whether grave unadulterated sin or lies to get out of work today. What does the devil come to do? Steal, kill, destroy. But eternal life comes with the kingdom of God. And it's free. And we have a choice. God will not force Himself on any of us. He is a gentleman. All we need to do is ask.

Once we do, EVERY promise is ours for the taking (see Chapter 6). That is no lie.

It is important to know that, as I explained before, the enemy, the devil, is a liar. He is full of lies and is "the father of lies." Tricks, lies, smokescreens—that is what he uses to deceive and convince people that he doesn't exist, that what the world has to offer is better than God. Don't believe him. "Submit yourselves therefore to God. Resist the devil, and he will flee from you" (James 4:7).

Sometimes it's the devil—a lot of the time. But sometimes it's the choices we make. As you look to God for answers and become familiar with Him and how the kingdom works, it becomes less and less of an issue to resist the devil. It becomes second nature to look to God for the answers instead of relying on ourselves and the worldly system. And we become account-able for our own actions and choices. "Therefore each of you must put off falsehood and speak truthfully to your neighbor, for we are all members of one body. In your anger do not sin: Do not let the sun go down while you are still angry, and *do not give the devil a foothold*" (Ephesians 4:25–27). Do not let him in. It gives him a legal right to wreak havoc in your life.

CHAPTER
16

GIVE, GIVE, GIVE

The kingdom of God works on a sowing and reaping principle. You sew seed; it is watered and fed with faith and belief and trust in God, and in due time, you reap the harvest. It may be a seed of love, comfort, assistance, time, money, etc. There are many seeds to plant throughout life.

Jesus taught us a lesson in Luke 8:5–15. Some seeds were sown in good rich soil, some in not so good soil. He tells us:

Now the parable is this: The seed is the word of God. Those by the wayside are the ones who hear; then the devil comes and takes away the word out of their hearts, lest they should believe and be saved. But the ones on the rock are those who, when they hear, receive the word with joy; and these have no root, who believe for a while and in time of temptation fall away. Now the ones that fell among thorns are those who, when they have heard, go out and are choked with cares, riches, and pleasures of life, and bring no fruit to maturity. But the ones that fell on the good ground are those who, having heard the word with a noble and good heart, keep it and bear fruit with patience.

We are the soil. How we cultivate or live will determine the harvest we will reap in time. Our heart and the drive behind our giving has everything to do with our receiving. God knows our heart and intentions.

> Each one must give as he has decided in his heart, not reluctantly or under compulsion, for God loves a cheerful giver.
>
> 2 Corinthians 9:7
>
> Give, and it will be given to you. Good measure, pressed down, shaken together, running over, will be put into your lap. For with the measure you use it will be measured back to you.
>
> Luke 6:38 ESV
>
> The point is this: whoever sows sparingly will also reap sparingly, and whoever sows bountifully will also reap bountifully.
>
> 2 Corinthians 9:6

Tithing is another principle or seed we sow. Some argue this is not for today. They say this is old testament living. We need to remember that Jesus didn't die on the Cross to abolish the law. He died so we no longer had to live under the constraints of the law. It doesn't mean that we still don't follow the principles and examples set in the old testament. Paul clarified what Jesus taught us: the Law shows us what God wants (holiness), and grace gives us the desire and power to be holy. We are not trusting in the Law; we are trusting in Christ. We are freed from the Law's bondage by His one-time sacrifice.

> What shall we say then? Are we to continue in sin that grace may abound? By no means! How can we who died to sin still live in it? Do you not know that all of us who have been baptized into Christ Jesus were baptized into his death? We were buried therefore with him by baptism into death, in order that, just as Christ was raised from the dead by the glory of the Father, we too might walk in newness of life.
>
> Romans 6:1–4

I learned somewhere that there is an equation to Faith = Believing + Trusting + Obeying. If any part of the equation is removed, we are attempting to grow by feelings instead of by faith.

Our giving is a part of our growth in the Lord. Meaning; we give, we love, we share, we sew into the kingdom. It is also how we represent our Savior and our loving God. Everywhere we go, people should be able to see the Jesus in us. And a by-product of that giving (in all areas) is to be blessed with the harvest.

If you are not receiving love, finances, comfort, time, etc., check your giving. Most likely you are lacking in that area.

CHAPTER 17

TRUST HIM

Within the formula of faith we just reviewed is trust. It is like oxygen. Without it you will fail. Trusting in God and all He says is the key to survival in daily life. We trust that God's Word is the absolute and unstained truth for how we are to live life. We trust that if God says He fights our battles for us, He is fighting our battles.

I have to admit, this was one of the hardest things for me to get wrapped around and into my head. It took time. Especially because I want to be in control of all things that go on in my life. I was that way most of my life. I still struggle. But the awesome thing there is that God forgives me. He knows. He understands. So I stop. Focus on what HE says. Move on.

It's 10:00 a.m. on a Monday morning and that person that consistently feels the need to compete and dig into your personal space is pushing your buttons again…with your boss… at the team meeting…in front of everyone. They even got a big laugh with a snide remark made at your expense. Oh man. You speak softly in your head, "Lord, help me. I need this job. Wait, You said, Lord, that YOU would fight my battles. YOU are my strength. YOU said I only need to be silent." And with that, you keep your mouth shut and smile. And thank God, He gives you strength to do so. What happens next is an example of WHY trusting God is the pooh. Your boss calls you to her office that very Monday and explains that you have made such great strides in dedication and portraying a professional and strong work ethic that she has chosen you for the big promotion you didn't even ask for. It is true. God works for you always.

Some might say that it was your choice to keep your mouth shut. It was you that decided to use constraint and move on—turn the other cheek. That may be. But the one who is serving the Lord and trusting in God KNOWS that your actions and choices, when based on the foundation of God's Word, take you higher, lend to the Kingdom, and are fueled by the power of the Holy Spirit in you. And, again, I know I don't want to do anything that would hurt my relationship with Jesus or stop my blessings. I trust that He has my back at ALL times. "For the Lord your God is he who goes with you to fight for you against your enemies, to give you the victory" (Deuteronomy 20:4). "The Lord will fight for you, and you have only to be silent" (Exodus 14:14).

Trusting in God's Word has put me over in life. Trust is the key ingredient in receiving those promises I had been believing for all along.

The definition of trust is a firm belief in the reliability, truth, ability, or strength of someone or something. Similar words are confidence, belief, faith, freedom from suspicion/doubt, sureness.

Think of it this way: trust and belief in God's Word are the bridge that bring the manifestation of promises from the spiritual world into the natural.

CHAPTER
18

OBEDIENCE CAN BE DIFFICULT

I'm not going to sit back and say things like, "Oh yeah, this is a piece of cake. I stroll through this without a care every day" because those would be bold-faced lies. Obedience, following God's Word and direction, can be difficult. It's not always a walk in the park.

The fact is, once the devil knows you are a threat to his kingdom and an asset to God's, you walk around with a target on your back. Not always, but it happens. "Indeed, all who desire to live a godly life in Christ Jesus will be persecuted" (2 Timothy 3:12).

It's easy to blow a gasket, pop off when you're mad, hold a grudge, take the wide path, and follow the ways of the enemy. It's easy to follow the ways of the world. We, as Christians, are a unique and peculiar people. And when the world is bending and removing God and feeding our youth the ways that do not conform to the Lord, it becomes a challenge to stand strong. Particularly when it all seems like such a humanitarian and loving thing to do, as it is presented by those who do not serve our Lord. First John 2:15–17 tells us:

> Do not love the world or the things in the world. If anyone loves the world, the love of the Father is not in him. For all that is in the world—the desires of the flesh and the desires of the eyes and pride of life— is not from the Father but is from the world. And

the world is passing away along with its desires, but whoever does the will of God abides forever.

For the time will come when they will not endure sound doctrine; but after their own lusts shall they heap to themselves teachers, having itching ears; And they shall turn away their ears from the truth, and shall be turned unto fables.

2 Timothy 4:3–4

God is our source. Not man. Not the world. We must stand strong in our beliefs and we do that by following the Word of God. We stay diligent in soaking up the truth, the Bible, the living breathing Word of God. Every answer to every problem in life is in the Bible. The more you know, the stronger you become in your walk. The more you are equipped to handle the daily trials of life.

My walk has become less of a struggle since my realization that God is for me, not against me. He fights my battles. "The LORD will fight for you, and you have only to be silent" (Exodus 14:14). It is much easier now to stop, shut my beak, and let God take over in a situation of animosity or confrontation, etc. than it was fifteen years ago. But there are times that it is a struggle. The kids are fighting, the husband is grumpy, you're late for work, and so on, and you feel like the world is crumbling and you want to explode. It is a trick, a lot of the time, by the enemy to get you off course. He wants to pull you away from the things of God. That way you won't receive those blessings and you will turn more and more to the ways of the world—the easy way—the way everyone else is going.

Think about it. When you watch an action film, you are expecting the good guy to blow up or eliminate the bad guy. It's the way of the world. The bad guy loses, the good guy gets the girl. What about today's society of revenge? The man cheats, the woman stalks and plans and seeks her revenge. We've all seen the billboard with the scorned wife's message to the cheating husband. This is not the Lord's way. Jesus told us in Luke 6:35, "But love your enemies, and do good, and lend, expecting nothing in return, and your reward will be great, and you will be sons of the Most High, for he is kind to the ungrateful and the evil." We have also been told in Matthew 22:37, "Thou shalt love the Lord thy God with all thy heart, and with all thy soul, and with all thy mind. This is the first and great commandment. And the second is like unto it, Thou shalt love thy neighbour as thyself." Not the first choice of most of today's world, thus the difficulty.

The way of the Lord is a narrow path and a difficult one at that. But we must, again, be the example. We must be the representatives of Jesus on this earth. Let them see the Jesus in you every day in everything you do, as difficult as that may be. We will reap the rewards for our dedication.

Do not be deceived: God is not mocked, for whatever one sows, that will he also reap.

Galatians 6:7

Do not neglect to do good and to share what you have, for such sacrifices are pleasing to God.

Hebrews 13:16

And let us not grow weary of doing good, for in due season we will reap, if we do not give up.

Galatians 6:9

That you may be blameless and innocent, children of God without blemish in the midst of a crooked and twisted generation, among whom you shine as lights in the world.

Philippians 2:15

Serving the Lord has changed my perspective and ability to perform under pressure as well as under fire. I am NOT, by any means, close to being able to turn the other cheek as quickly as I should. As a matter of fact, I struggle with letting things go sometimes because, let's face it, there are just a lot of "characters" or "button pushers" out there. Remember Scar from the *Lion King*, George from that '90s sitcom, the step mom from *Cinderella*, Merideth from the *Parent Trap*, Regina George

(Rizzo) from *Grease*—and the list goes on. They are all major button pushers. Some are people you see occasionally, some are family, some we deal with on a daily basis. It is difficult not to pop off, especially if you're tired or had a hard day. But I can tell you what my walk with the Lord has taught me. Even if I do falter in my steps, I repent immediately, and I pray for them like Jesus told us in Luke 6:35. And I remember how I've learned that it's not always the person, it can be the enemy USING that person. They don't have what I have and are missing out. They don't know what I know. So I pray for them.

CHAPTER
19

BE QUICK TO REPENT

Speaking of difficult, I mean, it was never the first thing on my mind when I was spouting off to whomever irritated me, to be quick to apologize or recognize that I was wrong. And if I could illuminate and emphasize the word "I" in the last sentence, I would.

And then I learned that in Luke 5:31, Jesus answered them, "It is not the healthy who need a doctor, but the sick. I have not come to call the righteous, but sinners to repentance." Acts 3:19: "Repent, then, and turn to God, so that your sins may be wiped out, that times of refreshing may come from the Lord." Yes, I would like that refreshing please.

"He who sins is of the devil, for the devil has sinned from the beginning. For this purpose the Son of God was manifested, that He might destroy the works of the devil" (1 John 3:8). So we see here that it is very important to repent quickly so we do not allow ourselves to become a slave to sin or to live like the enemy. We don't need sin or the enemy getting in the way of our blessings. "Whoever conceals his transgressions will not prosper, but he who confesses and forsakes them will obtain mercy" (Proverbs 28:13). "When you were slaves to sin, you were free from the obligation to do right" (Romans 6:20, NLT). Well, doing right is what I want to do now. I don't want to grieve the Holy Spirit. I want to be a blessing to the Lord and others.

I DO NOT want to contribute to hell, the devil, or death in any way, shape, or form. He is a liar and a thief and steals from those we love. The deceiver of the brethren:

> So the great dragon was cast out, that serpent of old, called the Devil and Satan, who deceives the whole world; he was cast to the earth, and his angels were cast out with him. Then I heard a loud voice saying in heaven, "Now salvation, and strength, and the kingdom of our God, and the power of His Christ have come, for the accuser of our brethren, who accused them before our God day and night, has been cast down. And they overcame him by the blood of the Lamb and by the word of their testimony, and they did not love their lives to the death.'"
>
> Revelation 12:11

Again, we are back to the knowledge of things, knowing what happens when you continue to sin (do wrong) or live in righteousness (do right). You have a choice and you will reap the reward of whichever you choose.

So you know, "repent" means to turn around.

CHAPTER
20

FORGIVE... YOU HAVE BEEN!

Ahhh, the story of the grudge-holder. "You don't know what I've been through with him!" "I'll never speak to them again as long as I live!" We've all been there. The unthinkable act, the pain and torment of the past, the hate for the sin that caused us that pain. It is a horrible thing to carry. And it really is the sin, not the person. But we must forgive.

Yes, people just don't always know, say, do, or move in a way that has YOUR best interest at heart. People are selfish. People carry evil within them as well. But the forgiveness isn't for them. It's for you.

I know how hard it is. Really. If I'm going to be 100 percent truthful, I can say that I have walked with a passionate hate for people that have stabbed me in the back and done things to cause me frustration and severe pain. I've had the rug pulled out from under me several times. And it still can be upsetting to think about. But…then came Jesus.

I love the Lord with such a passion that there is nothing that anyone on this earth can do to take my joy away. When I get upset, I stop. I get through the situation, give myself time, then focus on what God says about it. Sometimes immediately, sometimes not so quick. In the end, I always realize that the people who are hurting me are the ones who are missing out. They don't know what they are missing. They don't have the capability to feel and be surrounded with love and blessing like I do. So I pray for them. I pray that God will work on their hearts and they will learn. It's what Jesus would have done, so it's what I am going to do. Now, that is not to say that there isn't any repentance going on in the interim. I am still working on that. But the Word of God has guided me into the joy of forgiveness and takes that darkness out of me. Every time. Without fail. I love Him so much for that. Thank you, Lord.

God says in Ezekiel 36:25–27

> I will sprinkle clean water on you, and you shall be clean from all your uncleannesses, and from all your idols I will cleanse you. And I will give you a new heart, and a new spirit I will put within you. And I will remove the heart of stone from your flesh and give you a heart of flesh.

When you give your heart to Him, living in the love and forgiveness comes much easier, much quicker. Of course, we live in a world that can hurt us but, a heart that is receiving and giving the love of Christ is one that can forgive so much quicker. We have to remember: "Hatred stirs up strife, but love covers all offenses" (Proverbs 10:12).

Living with a grudge is like drinking the poison yourself and expecting the rat to die. It festers and builds and turns your heart hard.

If anyone says, "I love God," and hates his brother, he is a liar; for he who does not love his brother whom he has seen cannot love God whom he has not seen.

1 John 4:20

Be kind to one another, tender hearted, forgiving one another, as God in Christ forgave you.

Ephesians 4:32

Jesus told us in Luke 6:37:

Judge not, and you will not be judged; condemn not, and you will not be condemned; forgive, and you will be forgiven.

And again in Luke 6:27:

But I say to you who hear, Love your enemies, do good to those who hate you.

As you can read, unforgiveness is not only a poison to yourself and others, it will keep you out of heaven. Mark 11:25–26 Jesus said, "Whenever you stand praying, if you have anything against anyone, forgive him, that your Father in heaven may also forgive you your trespasses. But if you do not forgive, neither will your Father in heaven forgive your trespasses."

We have to remember to let God take the wheel in all aspects of life. Forgiveness is another aspect we should hand off to Him. Ask Him to help you. He will.

CHAPTER
21

THE BATTLE HAS BEEN WON

That is past-tense. We are the victors here. This is another fact that has to get down into your spirit, soul, and body. Jesus took it all at the Cross, on our behalf. The book of Romans has a lot to say about it all:

No, in all these things we are more than conquerors through him who loved us.

Romans 8:37 (NIV)

What then shall we say to these things? If God is for us, who can be against us?

Romans 8:31

There is therefore now no condemnation for those who are in Christ Jesus. For the law of the Spirit of life has set you free in Christ Jesus from the law of sin and death. For God has done what the law, weakened by the flesh, could not do. By sending his own Son in the likeness of sinful flesh and for sin, he condemned sin in the flesh, in order that the righteous require-ment of the law might be fulfilled in us, who walk not according to the flesh but according to the Spirit. For those who live according to the flesh set their minds on the things of the flesh, but those who live according to the Spirit set their minds on the things of the Spirit.

Romans 8:1–39

There is power in knowledge. Knowing that you are the victor and that Christ has already defeated the enemy is a huge game changer when faced with adversities. "I can do all things through Christ which strengtheneth me" (Philippians 4:13, KJV). Go back to the example of the snarky coworker. The power was in KNOWING that the Lord is your strength and that He has your back at all times. "Because you have made the Lord, who is my refuge, Even the Most High, your dwelling place, No evil shall befall you, Nor shall any plague come near your dwelling" (Psalms 91: 9–10, NKJV).

The whole premise of Psalm 91 is that when you abide in the presence of God there is safety. This is a scripture I know well and speak over my family regularly. Dig in. It is so beautiful. The love and gifts He bestows upon us are wonderful.

Walk knowing the truth about the victory. It is done. The enemy is a failure. He lost the battle to Jesus and his time here on earth is short. He tries consistently to take down as many of us as he can, BUT if you know…KNOW…who you are in Christ, Who won the battle, what God says about you, then the fire isn't quite so hot when you walk through it. The trials that we all experience will continue to refine and mold you to become the person God has created you to be. You are victorious.

It may seem like the trouble is never going to end, or that the battle has been ongoing for as long as you can remember, but there is a reason for it. It may not make sense now. It may not be until way in the future that you realize why you walked in turmoil. It may not be until we are in heaven. But there is a reason. "And we know that God causes all things to work together for good to those who love God, to those who are called according to His purpose" (Romans 8:28). "There is an appointed time for everything. And there is a time for every event under heaven" (Ecclesiastes 3:1). I have found in my walk so far, the things that I have battled have given me knowledge and strength in order to assist someone else walking in that very same thing.

Although we do walk through trials, we remain the victors. Walk in that knowledge always. Jesus told us in Matthew in 5:10–12, "Blessed are those who are persecuted because of righteousness, for theirs is the kingdom of heaven. Blessed are you when people insult you, persecute you and falsely say all kinds of evil against you because of me." I don't expect it. But I do handle it so much better now, knowing the Lord fights for us and we are the winners.

The disciples walked through the fire for Christ. Most of them met very violent deaths for their dedication in spreading the word of repentance and Christ. They stayed their course for their beliefs and to be sure the truth was told. And we know that their reward in heaven is great. "Rejoice and be glad, for your reward in heaven is great; for in the same way they persecuted the prophets who were before you" (Matthew 5:12). "For the

Son of Man is going to come in the glory of His Father with His angels, and will then repay every man according to his deeds" (Matthew 16:27).

CHAPTER
22

BE A BELIEVER WITH A RECEIVER

Remember the dial up radios? We still have them in our cars but not quite like when I was young. A radio/stereo system in the living room in a fancy cabinet where you had to switch from AM to FM and turn the dial to tune in to the station you wanted. Or a small transistor you took with you on a hike or fishing. You clicked them on, dialed in, and received the signal you were looking for.

How's your receiver? Are you tuned in to pick up the fine-tuned frequency of all the crisp, clean, and revelatory knowledge being sent out here, in church, reading your Bible, etc.? Your receiver has to be on at all times. Pick up the knowledge daily, whether it be one chapter in a book of the Bible, one scripture, one podcast, whatever. You must be filled up every day with the knowledge of the Word of God. Once received, the word of knowledge can grow and flourish and help you and others. It is like oxygen. We breathe and that oxygen feeds all the parts of our bodies to keep us alive. Without it, we die.

Without the Word of God, we die. "My people perish for lack of knowledge" (Hosea 4:6). God never wanted it to be like this. He gave us His Word to save ourselves. Ignorance is a horribly destructive state. Many souls have perished because of a lack of knowledge. But God never wanted it to be, so that is why He gave us His Word. As we receive and believe the Word and let it grow inside of us, we take it out to share with others to stop as many as possible from perishing. "I call heaven and earth to witness against you today, that I have set before you life and death, the blessing and the curse. So choose life in order that you may live, you and your descendants" (Deuteronomy 30:19). Choose to receive Life and the Word and all the promises of God.

Belief...

> And without faith it is impossible to please him, for whoever would draw near to God must believe that he exists and that he rewards those who seek him.
>
> Hebrews 11:6
>
> Therefore I tell you, whatever you ask in prayer, believe that you have received it, and it will be yours.
>
> Mark 11:24

Believe and receive my brothers and sisters. Believe and receive.

> For God so loved the world, that he gave his only Son, that whoever believes in him should not perish but have eternal life.
>
> John 3:16

Remember when I stated that, as Christians, we are a peculiar people? Well, we are! We are not a seeing is believing kind of people. We actually go in the opposite direction. We believe in the things we cannot see. "Jesus said to him, "Have you believed because you have seen me? Blessed are those who have not seen and yet have believed" (John 20:29). As much as I would have loved to have walked with and seen the miracles firsthand with Jesus, I don't need to. I know He is with me; I know He is real; I know I have the knowledge and ability to receive the promises He has for us all, right here, right now. I do believe so I have received! It is so powerful.

CHAPTER
23

THE NARROW PATH

The choice to serve God is one that will lead you from the path of unknown destruction to paradise. We live in times that are leading us to destruction. The things that were not accepted just four or five decades ago are now acceptable and encouraged. Choices that lead good people to their deaths are publicized, pushed through our government leaders, and accepted by unknowing and ignorant people. Ignorant in the knowledge of spiritual life and death. "Enter through the narrow gate. For wide is the gate and broad is the road that leads to destruction, and many enter through it. But small is the gate and narrow the road that leads to life, and only a few find it" (Matthew 7:13–14).

If there is anything that I have learned throughout life, it is that the choices we make will lead us to success or failure. If we make wise choices, if we dig in and search for the answers instead of just going with the flow and letting someone else do it for us, we will end up with a much more rewarding and satisfying close. Those choices are not always easy. They take dedication and persistence. I can tell you now, with complete and absolute assurance, that the road to life, and life abundantly, includes serving God. Choose life.

God is our Creator. He is an omnipotent, omniscient, and all-powerful Being who spoke our world and us into existence. He created us to worship Him. We are not here by accident. You are not here by accident. You were chosen to live in this present day and time to fulfill a purpose designed by our Creator. You are reading this book at this present time for a specific reason. "But you are a chosen race, a royal priesthood, a holy nation, a people for his own possession, that you may proclaim the excellencies of him who called you out of darkness into his marvelous light" (1 Peter 2:9). "You did not choose me, but I chose you and appointed you that you should go and bear fruit and that your fruit should abide, so that whatever you ask the Father in my name, he may give it to you" (John 15:16). Do you want to be a fruit bearer and live on into eternity or live for the short here and now and head to your death? The choice is all yours.

Think about some of the most intricate and beautiful creations. The wildflower, with its ability to produce pollen, and the bee that knows instinctively how to gather it and take it back to create the honey. The sky in all its beauty and wondrous colors, blues, oranges, yellows, pinks. Incredible! The beauty of an early summer morning over the mountain top with mist laying on the open fields and gorgeous soft light parading through the peaks. The intricacies of the ability of the human body to adapt and heal itself. These wonders and so many more are not a product of a mysterious explosion in the middle of the universe. There is no other explanation but our God. Even science is now turning to the truth in finding that life must include an actual Creator. Do your research. Check into the shroud or cloth that was covering Jesus' face and what has been found out about it. It's amazing.

The point of this chapter is to let you know that there is a Creator, and He is in love with you, but it is not always the easiest choice to make to serve Him. There is nothing that you have done or will do (with the exception of blaspheming the Holy Spirit*) in this life that He will not forgive, and there is no other God that is alive and waiting for us all to choose Him so we don't perish. But the enemy makes it easy to sin. Everybody else is doing it. Why not go with the flow? Death is why. Hell is why. Reaping the gifts and benefits of serving God is why. Blessing our children with the same is why. Living with the blanket of love and protection of our Lord is why.

You DO NOT have to live with anxiety, fear of what's next, impoverished, sick, suffering, or with any other curse that causes you anguish and pain. Jesus became all of that and more on the Cross FOR US so we don't have to live that way. He did all the suffering FOR US. "Christ hath redeemed us from the curse of the law, being made a curse for us: for it is written, Cursed is everyone that hangeth on a tree" (Galatians 3:13).

*Blaspheming the Holy Spirit: "Truly I tell you, people can be forgiven all their sins and every slander they utter, but whoever blasphemes against the Holy Spirit will never be forgiven; they are guilty of an eternal sin" (Mark 3:28–30, NIV). He said this because they were saying, "He has an impure spirit." Billy Graham advised this along with referencing one study Bible: "To commit this sin one must consciously, persistently, deliberately, and maliciously reject the testimony of the Spirit to the deity and saving power of the Lord Jesus." If a person keeps doing that until death, there is no hope of forgiveness and eternal life in heaven.

CHAPTER 24

BUT MAN WROTE IT

I've heard this several times and been questioned about the origin of the Word of God, the Bible. "Man wrote the Bible—how can I trust that it is real?" I want to expound on this just a bit more.

Chapter 7 reviews what the Word of God says about this. Scripture was inspired by God, who used man, to write down the truth of God's Word. I, myself, had the very same questions before I was saved.

The very book you are reading right now is God-inspired. The Holy Spirit has impressed upon me and given me ideas, thoughts, and words to put down on paper to share with you. It is something that only those who truly want to know, feel, and experience—FROM THEIR HEART—will experience.

There are those that argue this over and over. There is someone reading this right now that just said that in a conversation recently held with a believer. Although you are not a believer, the Holy Spirit is speaking to you through me. That is how it works. We are God's hands and feet. We do the work for Him, as His disciples, to save as many people as we can from going to hell and receiving death instead of life.

Why doesn't God just wave His hand and make us all believers right now? Because it's the law. The spiritual world is all very legalistic. God cannot go against His own laws or there would be very dire consequences for the world. His ways are not our ways.

Let the wicked forsake his way and the unrighteous man his thoughts; and let him return to the Lord, and He will have love, pity, and mercy for him, and to our God, for He will multiply to him His abundant pardon. For My thoughts are not your thoughts, neither are your ways My ways, says the Lord. For as the heavens are higher than the earth, so are My ways higher than your ways and My thoughts than your thoughts. For as the rain and snow come down from the heavens, and return not there again, but water the earth and make it bring forth and sprout, that it may give seed to the sower and bread to the eater, So shall My word be that goes forth out of My mouth: it shall not return to Me void [without producing any effect, useless], but it shall accomplish that which I please and purpose, and it shall prosper in the thing for which I sent it.

Isaiah 55: 7–11

Then said the Lord to me, You have seen well, for I am alert and active, watching over My word to perform it.

Jeremiah 1:12 (AMP)

I implore you to humble yourself, lose the haughtiness, open your heart and your mind, and really seek the truth. He will reveal Himself to you. But it is up to you. When you carry doubt and mistrust and turn up your nose with unbelief, you will gain nothing.

Seriously. Why are you reading this book right now? You want answers, whether you are serving the Lord or not. You seek the Truth. Although your life may be full of great things, great job, family, and more, there is or was something missing. Deep down, you seek out something that will give you peace and fulfillment. A hole somewhere in there that is or was nagging at you and causes separation, anxiety, fear, doubt, negativity, and so on. Oh, it's all great when you're young and living for good times and yourself but, when the seriousness of life kicks in, it hits you in one way or another. Everyone has it. Remember the story of how I knew not to move forward at that stop light? It's in you as well. You may or may not listen to it, but it's there. Open up your heart. Ask and ye shall receive.

Psalm 19 reveals:

> The heavens declare the glory of God, and the sky above proclaims his handiwork. Day to day pours out speech, and night to night reveals knowledge. There is no speech, nor are there words, whose voice is not heard. Their voice goes out through all the earth, and their words to the end of the world. In them he has set a tent for the sun, which comes out like a bride-

groom leaving his chamber, and, like a strong man, runs its course with joy. Its rising is from the end of the heavens, and its circuit to the end of them, and there is nothing hidden from its heat.

My personal belief is that the world lacks respect. We had less turmoil and more fear of God when there was evidence of respect. People understood that God comes first. The reverence and "fear of God" is just that. Respect. Honor. Obedience for the truth and an intolerance for sin.

The enemy came in and slowly picked apart the respect and honor. He made it so people live for how they feel instead of what is right. How do I know what is right? The Word of God tells us. Man has walked right into the devil's trap and deception. And now we, as Christians, are persecuted in every direction.

It's all laid out for us in the Word. It's predicted:

> For men shall be lovers of their own selves, covetous, boasters, proud, blasphemers, disobedient to parents, unthankful, unholy, 3 Without natural affection, trucebreakers, false accusers, incontinent, fierce, despisers of those that are good, 4 Traitors, heady, highminded, lovers of pleasures more than lovers of God.
>
> 2 Timothy 3:2-4 (KJV)

Man wrote it by the physical act of putting it down on paper, but it is God's Word.

You are not smarter than God.

CHAPTER

25

"BUT I'M A GOOD PERSON"– DON'T FALL FOR THAT

You know, the devil isn't opposed to good people. He doesn't have to fight them off or worry about them taking souls to heaven. Good people are everywhere. Good people live their daily lives helping their neighbors and working charities and doing good deeds everywhere. But good people go to hell every day.

Why, you ask? Well, so far, we have covered quite a bit, including respect, fear of God, belief, and obedience, among other topics related to a spirit-filled life. I go the long way around to ensure that it sinks in for you and you understand that there is one way and ONLY ONE WAY to get to heaven.

Do not let your hearts be troubled. You believe in God; believe also in me. My Father's house has many rooms; if that were not so, would I have told you that I am going there to prepare a place for you? And if I go and prepare a place for you, I will come back and take you to be with me that you also may be where I am. You know the way to the place where I am going." Thomas said to him, "Lord, we don't know where you are going, so how can we know the way?" Jesus answered, "I am the way and the truth and the life. **No one comes to the Father except through me**. If you really know me, you will know my Father as well. From now on, you do know him and have seen him."

John 14

The very short and loose explanation is this: God created heaven and paradise on earth. He put us in it to worship and live for Him. The enemy was kicked out of heaven for exalting himself above God. He saw we were created to worship God (which was his job originally) and stepped in to trick us and sin began. God even sent His only Son to save us from our sin and we still mess it up. WE have fallen for the lies and deception and the closer we get to the return of Jesus, the worse it becomes. All of this is our own doing, by the way. God set us up and we couldn't follow one simple rule. God leaves it up to us. He gives us all a choice. "Therefore each of you must put off falsehood and speak truthfully to your neighbor, for we are all members of one body. In your anger do not sin: Do not let the sun go down while you are still angry, and do not give the devil a foothold" Ephesians 4:25–27. In other words, don't let the enemy in to wreak havoc—legally—when you sin, you let him in.

Hell wasn't created for us. It was created for the devil and his followers. We make the choices that take us there. God set up the universe—the world and all its wonder and majesty for us, but there are laws, spiritual and natural. We must obey them to keep the sin and destruction out. The same as in the natural world we live in. People KNOW that there are laws that have to be followed or there would be chaos. But believing in another world with rules seems to be an issue.

That is, again, a very, very loose description of spirit and natural world order. But I tell you this to explain that once sin came in, we blew it. When you allow sin to run you, it takes you to an eternity of torture and destruction. There are plenty of testimonies of people who have had near-death experiences and speak about what hell is like. You don't want this.

The quest for spiritual answers is what led me here today. I was fascinated by the spiritual world, having had spiritual experiences of my own. I watched true ghost stories and listened to people's testimonies of their "hauntings" and whatnot. I was pulled in different directions until the Lord led me to where He wanted me. And here I am. I was always a good person. I wouldn't hurt anyone, ever, intentionally. I didn't know what I know now. I didn't know I was headed for destruction. But I know now what I want, the direction I need to be heading, and how to live to ensure I make it to heaven. My life is so enriched and the Lord has blessed me beyond what I could ever imagine. Thank you, Lord. I want that for you. I am here to help you to understand and save you from hell. I pray that you are touched by the Lord and receive His love now. I pray you seek Him out.

Don't fall for the devil's lies and deception. And I can tell you, at this very moment, if you are not serving the Lord, you are being filled with overwhelming doubt. Resist it! "Submit yourselves therefore to God. Resist the devil, and he will flee from you" (James 4:7). He came to steal, kill, and destroy. There is no other purpose for him than to take you away from the Lord and make it all seem unbelievable. "The natural person does not accept the things of the Spirit of God, for they are folly to him, and he is not able to understand them because they are spiritually discerned" (1 Corinthians 2:14). (Also, see Chapter 15.)

Again, I say *don't fall for it!* You have a manual for life at your disposal. Use it.

CHAPTER
26

YOU'RE NOT "ONLY HUMAN"

The "natural person" in Christian terms is the one who is not serving the Lord. Once you are born again, your spirit is as clean and pure as Jesus. There's nothing you can do about it. You are a three-part being: a spirit enclothed in a soul (mind, will, and emotion) enclothed in a body (your flesh). I've heard the body described as an earth suit.

There are fantastic studies out there that will break down the three parts, far greater than I have the ability to do. But for now, read some of what the Word of God says and ask Him to open your eyes:

> But I say, walk by the Spirit, and you will not gratify the desires of the flesh. For the desires of the flesh are against the Spirit, and the desires of the Spirit are against the flesh, for these are opposed to each other, to keep you from doing the things you want to do.
>
> Galatians 5:16–17
>
> May God himself, the God of peace, sanctify you through and through. May your whole spirit, soul and body be kept blameless at the coming of our Lord Jesus Christ.
>
> 1 Thessalonians 5:23 (NIV)

Man has a history of just screwing things up. Seriously, we have a hard time sharing toilet paper, let alone making the choice for life instead of death, even when the truth is presented to everyone in one way or another. And it HAS BEEN. We tend to make the destructive choice. But that doesn't mean you consistently chalk it up to the "only human" excuse. We have been given an instruction manual for life. The choice for Christ is one that will open your eyes and heart to the truth and help you to live a fulfilling and prosperous life with less of the sin (screwing it up) and more blessing. And an eternity to enjoy and not perish.

Yes, sometimes we do make mistakes and yes, we are human and by nature want to be greedy and live for ourselves, but when you make the choice to let the Lord be your Savior, to open your heart and your life to the love and promises of God, life takes the most amazing turn. The focus moves from you to Him. The destructive ways of living for the world dissipate. You no longer want to do things, say things, and live in a way that will hurt you or those around you, even if you didn't realize that's what you were doing. The choices you make will be considered with the things God wants for you. And let me tell you, there is not one thing, NOTHING you can ever imagine or think of that is better than what God has in store for you.

Human is defined in Britannica as "human being, a culture-bearing primate classified in the genus Homo, especially the species H. sapiens. Human beings are anatomically similar and related to the great apes but are distinguished by a more highly developed brain and a resultant capacity for articulate speech and abstract reasoning."

Fun fact: I had to rewrite several sarcastic ape remarks at this point because of my human brain and tendency to "lay it on thick" at times. I'll let you use your imaginations and move on.

Spirit defined in the Oxford Languages dictionary:

> the nonphysical part of a person which is the seat of emotions and character; the soul. "We seek a harmony between body and spirit"; the nonphysical part of a person regarded as their true self and as capable of surviving physical death or separation; the nonphysical part of a person manifested as an apparition after their death; a ghost; a supernatural being; the Holy Spirit.

Soul defined in Oxford Languages dictionary:

> the spiritual or immaterial part of a human being or animal, regarded as immortal. "they believe death is just one step in a soul's journey through the universe"

Three definitions listed but really, the soul and spirit define the two as the same thing because it is a worldview. Not God's definition.

Now I will go back to the earth suit. One of our pastors spoke about how eternity is like a beach that goes on forever.

The grains of sand are eternity and only one of those grains is your time here on earth. I like that analogy. You are wearing your earth suit while you are living out that one little grain. Your body wants to use that highly developed human brain to have fun, work, and live a great life. Your soul is kind of directing it with your choices and is defining and giving evidence of what type of person you are to lead you in those choices. But your spirit is something else. It is tied directly to God, Jesus, and the Holy Spirit. Without it, we cannot express the love of God.

So you are not only human after all. And once tapped into the spirit, you are a powerful three part being.

CHAPTER
27

CONFIRMATION

Today was church service. And what a service it was. I received confirmation of chapters in this book I just worked on yesterday, what the Lord was saying to me this morning, and that I am standing on the right scripture for something I am believing for.

Confirmation is something the Lord does through others and/or things you may see or hear. He may speak a word to you and then the next thing you know, you are hearing the same thing through your pastor, or friend, or on TV, or somewhere else. It tells you that you are on the right track and you were hearing or feeling correctly. "And they went forth, and preached everywhere, the Lord working with them, and confirming the word by the signs that followed. Amen" (Mark 16:20, ASV).

I've been in church service and felt the extreme need to walk over and give someone a twenty-dollar bill. And then find out that they drove in on fumes and didn't know how they were going to make it home without running out of gas. A stranger, mind you, that I probably would have only made a cordial hello to without the Lord's prompting. That is faith by that person to know God was going to provide for their need! And that is obedience to God's Word and confirmation that what I heard or felt was correct.

One day at work I was drifting off thinking of things when suddenly I had a vision of an aerial view above my church. There was a huge man about 2–3 stories tall standing outside the church. He looked like a warrior all dressed in garb, but I knew he was an angel there to protect and preserve the flow of the Holy Spirit. I instantly dismissed it. I actually thought that I was making this up in my head; that it was my imagination. I didn't tell anyone what I saw. A few weeks later, a woman at our church gave a long testimony of a vision she had written down to share with us all. She spoke about a huge angel she saw standing outside the church and described him to a tee. THAT is an exciting confirmation.

These types of incidents go on all the time. Christians hear and see and feel these confirmations almost daily. God works this way to help us but also to feed our faith, build us up, add excitement and wonder, and to keep us on track. But we aren't all tuned in. The world gets in the way. We have to focus, dedicate our time daily, and put God first in all we do in order to experience the wonders and fascinating things He has for us. He has to be your source for every need. He WILL confirm you are on the right path.

CHAPTER
28

BELIEVING IS SEEING

Believing in something you can't always see is the opposite of how the world walks and lives. "The proof is in the pudding." "I'll believe it when I see it." And then when miracles DO happen, we hear things like, "I can't believe my eyes."

Where would we be if Eve didn't feed Adam that apple? It would be every day, no second thoughts, living the dream, supernatural walking with God, fabulous never stop believing proof, and we wouldn't bat an eye.

Science adds to this. Scientific people have to see and break it down and get to the root of how it works. That is a fabulous way to get it done, whatever it may be. But as Christians, we live for a God we cannot see. We have faith, or believe, in a Creator that is an omnipotent, all-powerful Being.

It takes strength and determination in today's world to seek out a God you cannot see. But let me tell you this: it is so worth it. I have seen things that I never would have believed could happen! The difference in my life before and after serving God is one that I cannot explain in full detail. All I can tell you is that my life is so much more enriched and full and loved. I would never go back. I am so overwhelmed with the blessings and love of God that I want everyone to share in the same.

I believe. I know without a doubt that my God lives. I know with every breath I breathe that my God is alive and leading and guiding me through the good and the bad in my life. My belief—as it has grown and flourished—has brought me into the miraculous. The life I now live is 100 percent a full example of Job 8:7: "Though thy beginning was small, yet thy latter end should greatly increase." I have believed in the promises of God's Word and I now live and walk in them.

Again I say, remember: Faith and Belief are the Bridge that manifests the promises from the Spirit into the natural. We live in the natural world in our "earth suits" (that cracks me up). We have the ability to receive ALL the promises that God lays out in His Word right here, right now. Don't ever forget that.

CHAPTER
29

DROP THE IDOLS—DROP THE "FAKE"

There was a sorcerer named Simon you will find mentioned in the book of Acts. He wanted the power that was working through the disciples in their healing and helping of others. This particular sorcerer was very well known and very powerful. He was in such awe of the power working through the disciples that he tried to buy it from them.

> Now for some time a man named Simon had practiced sorcery in the city and amazed all the people of Samaria. He boasted that he was someone great, and all the people, both high and low, gave him their attention and exclaimed, "This man is rightly called the Great Power of God."
>
> Acts 8: 9–10

Then after Peter had laid hands and healed a local, Simon wanted what they had.

> When Simon saw that the Spirit was given at the laying on of the apostles' hands, he offered them money and said, "Give me also this ability so that everyone on whom I lay my hands may receive the Holy Spirit."
>
> Acts 8: 18–19

THE 411 SPIRIT-FILLED HANDBOOK

There is nothing higher or more powerful than the Power of God. You can look at all the things the world has to offer, like card readings, witchcraft, crystals, the earth, whatever. It is, and never will be, a power above that of God and the Holy Spirit working through you. Seriously. Ditch the rabbit's foot. Gross.

There is a pretty famous ex-satanist that has converted his love of power and hate to that of the love of Jesus. He gives testimony after testimony of how he was dedicated to the devil as a child. His parents served the wickedness and darkness, and he too fell into that world that continued to pull him in deeper and deeper. He had the ability to perform spells and rituals that would hurt and hinder others. The one thing that he states that is full of the wondrous truth of God is that he could not penetrate the light and love of a Christian. He could "see" the light emanating from them and how when he approached the Christian there was a powerful field or force around them that was impenetrable with his power. I believe every single word of it.

When I was young, we would have sleepover birthday parties and all of the girls would sit around in a circle and someone would lie in the middle with their arms folded over like a corpse. We all would use two fingers from each hand to lift that person while we were chanting some very real witchy chant. We didn't know. We were kids. It worked. They were light as a feather. I remember at my friend Julie's house the rest of the night I didn't feel right. It was eerie. We played with

Ouija boards and chanted in mirrors to spook each other and thought it was fun. We didn't know that we were allowing those dark spirits to enter our lives. Jesus told us in Luke 1:79, "to give light to those who sit in darkness and in the shadow of death, to guide our feet into the way of peace." That is part of why He came. We allow the darkness in and we "sit in the shadow of death."

These things are very real. The Bible tells us in Leviticus 19:31, "Do not turn to mediums or necromancers; do not seek them out, and so make yourselves unclean by them: I am the Lord your God." Manasseh, the King of Judah, was an early example of what not to do in 2 Chronicles 33:6, "He sacrificed his children in the fire in the Valley of Ben Hinnom, practiced divination and witchcraft, sought omens, and consulted mediums and spiritists. He did much evil in the eyes of the Lord, arousing his anger." Manesseh eventually figured out, with the help of the Lord, that our God is the only God and he removed all of the false idols and worked for and served the Lord. "Outside are the dogs and sorcerers and the sexually immoral and murderers and idolaters, and everyone who loves and practices falsehood" Revelation 22:15. Falsehood being the key term in that passage. Fake.

The devil has quite a practice out there. His worshipers have branched out into numerous areas and fool good people into believing the practice or mystical presentation is the way to go. Or that it will bring you "peace and harmony." It is a full truckload of crap! Do you remember WHO he is? "You belong to your father, the devil, and you want to carry out your father's desires. He was a murderer from the beginning, not holding to the truth, for there is no truth in him. When he lies, he speaks his native language, for he is a liar and the father of lies" (John 8:44). What does he come to do? "The thief comes only to steal and kill and destroy; I have come that they may have life, and have it to the full" (John 10:10).

The deception is a constant. It never stops. Crystals DO NOT give you peace and harmony. Our peace comes from the Lord. Period. Every wicked thing out there is disguised to fool you and to pull you in and to get you to ALLOW them into your life to wreak havoc, drop some illness on you, cause you fear, anxiety, lack, pain, and suffering. Fake! "For we do not wrestle against flesh and blood, but against the rulers, against the authorities, against the cosmic powers over this present darkness, against the spiritual forces of evil in the heavenly places" (Ephesians 6:12).

There is a spiritual world all around us and the good and the evil can see you and watch you protecting you or plotting against you. King David wrote so much about the protection and love of the Lord:

> The Lord is my light and my salvation; whom shall I
> fear? The Lord is the stronghold of my life; of whom

shall I be afraid? When evildoers assail me to eat up my flesh, my adversaries and foes, it is they who stumble and fall. Though an army encamp against me, my heart shall not fear; though war arise against me, yet I will be confident. One thing have I asked of the Lord, that will I seek after: that I may dwell in the house of the Lord all the days of my life, to gaze upon the beauty of the Lord and to inquire in his temple. For he will hide me in his shelter in the day of trouble; he will conceal me under the cover of his tent; he will lift me high upon a rock.

Psalm 27:1–14

For he will command his angels concerning you to guard you in all your ways.

Psalm 91:11

At one point in time, the King of Aram was trying to invade and come against the King of Israel. Elisha the prophet would advise the King of Israel just in time *every* time and the enemy's plans were thwarted.

"None of us, my lord the king," said one of his officers, "but Elisha, the prophet who is in Israel, tells the king of Israel the very words you speak in

> your bedroom." "Go, find out where he is," the king ordered, "so I can send men and capture him." The report came back: "He is in Dothan." Then he sent horses and chariots and a strong force there. They went by night and surrounded the city. When the servant of the man of God got up and went out early the next morning, an army with horses and chariots had surrounded the city. "Oh no, my lord! What shall we do?" the servant asked. "Don't be afraid," the prophet answered. *"Those who are with us are more than those who are with them."* And Elisha prayed, "Open his eyes, Lord, so that he may see." Then the Lord opened the servant's eyes, and he looked and saw the hills full of *horses and chariots of fire all around Elisha.*
>
> 2 Kings 6:12–17

My hand is raised for the horses and chariots of fire. The fruit is for the children, and that includes the protection. You do not need any other useless lies that the enemy is using to trick you. Personally, I don't like being tricked or fooled or lied to. I don't think any of us do. So my intention has always been to get to the truth. Well, here we are. Welcome! I'm praying for you now and I speak the truth of 2 Kings 6:17 over you now! Let your eyes see ONLY the truth!

"Idolatry, sorcery, enmity, strife, jealousy, fits of anger, rivalries, dissensions, divisions, envy, drunkenness, orgies, and things like these. I warn you, as I warned you before, that those who do such things will not inherit the kingdom of God" (Galatians 5:20–21). Steer clear of these things. Don't be fooled. And if you are not sure, GO WITH THE PEACE! And seek these gifts from above: "But the fruit of the Spirit is love, joy, peace, forbearance, kindness, goodness, faithfulness, gentleness and self-control. Against such things there is no law" (Galatians 5:22).

Your answers are in the Word of God. Your protection is in the Word. When you are armed with the truth and knowledge of what He says for and about you, then nothing can penetrate your peace, your love, your work, your family, your life. If it is from God, it will go along with His Word. If not, ditch it! Lose the Fake!

CHAPTER
30

SIN = LETTING HIM IN

The last chapter was a great segue into this topic. It is extremely important that you get this. Sin, or anything that goes against God's Word, will allow the enemy into your life. "Whoever makes a practice of sinning is of the devil, for the devil has been sinning from the beginning. The reason the Son of God appeared was to destroy the works of the devil" (1 John 3:8). "Be sober-minded; be watchful. Your adversary the devil prowls around like a roaring lion, seeking someone to devour" (1 Peter 5:8).

We talked about how the bad things happening in the world are not from God. The enemy, the devil, has been given a short time to run around the earth and sucker as many souls as he can into following him. His time is running out, and as the Word of God has predicted, the world is falling for his lies and schemes. "For people will love only themselves and their money. They will be boastful and proud, scoffing at God, disobedient to their parents, and ungrateful. They will consider nothing sacred" (2 Timothy 3:2 (NLT).

Sin, again, is going against God. Doing or saying things that would go against His Word and grieve His Holy Spirit and hurt your relationship with Him. "Know ye not that the unrighteous shall not inherit the kingdom of God? Be not deceived: neither fornicators, nor idolaters, nor adulterers, nor effeminate, nor abusers of themselves with mankind, Nor thieves, nor covetous, nor drunkards, nor revilers, nor extortioners, shall inherit the kingdom of God" (1 Corinthians 6:9). "But your iniquities have made a separation between you and your God, and your sins have hidden his face from you so that he does not hear" (Isaiah 59:2). Believe me, the love of God is something you don't ever want to lose. It is so very precious and something you never want to take for granted.

You have the power to overcome the world (sin and the devil). "For everyone who has been born of God overcomes the world. And this is the victory that has overcome the world—our faith" (1 John 5:4). "Put on the whole armor of God, that you may be able to stand against the schemes of the devil" (Ephesians 6:11). Your faith and belief in Jesus and the Word of God will keep you up and give you the power and knowledge you need to succeed!

Be quick to repent. We do make mistakes. I am good at it. But I can tell you that I am so very conscious of the fact that it is hindering me and my relationship with the Lord that almost instantly, I recognize it and apologize. "Just so, I tell you, there is joy before the angels of God over one sinner who repents" (Luke 15:10).

Carry yourself with the fear of the Lord. "The fear of the Lord is hatred of evil. Pride and arrogance and the way of evil and perverted speech I hate" (Proverbs 8:13). It is all around us, easy to take in and spew out at any given moment. But when you have the seeds planted inside, the Word and truth of God inside you, it rises up in times of need, in times of battle, and when you think you can't take one more step.

It is much harder to move forward with the things of the past when your heart is right with God. The Holy Spirit within you will give you that "gnawing" or feeling of dread or remorse much quicker than when you didn't have the Lord in your heart. Follow that unction. It will never lead you in the wrong direction. It will save you from making decisions that can block your blessings. Remember, God cannot look upon evil: "Your eyes are too pure to look on evil; you cannot tolerate wrongdoing. Why then do you tolerate the treacherous? Why are you silent while the wicked swallow up those more righteous than themselves?" (Habakkuk 1:13, NIV). How, then, would He be able to bless you?

The truth will always prevail. The light will always outshine the darkness. Keep that in you and walk knowing you are the victor at every turn. Even when you do those things that pull you in the wrong direction, be quick to apologize and He will be faithful to forgive you. EVERY time. Keep your heart and your head pointed in His direction and He will lead you where He wants you. That would be to blessings and unimaginable joy and peace. His plan far surpasses anything we could ever imagine for ourselves. Don't ever forget that.

CHAPTER
31

LOSE OFFENSE

The quickest and easiest way to stop the Lord's messengers from delivering your blessings and answers to prayers is to hold a grudge. I know, again with the forgiveness but, it really is very important for you to understand.

A brother offended is more unyielding than a strong city, and quarreling is like the bars of a castle.

Proverbs 18:19

Great peace have those who love your law; nothing can make them stumble.

Psalm 119:165

And if he sins against you seven times in the day, and turns to you seven times, saying, "I repent," you must forgive him.

Luke 17:4

And more insightful direction:

Repay no one evil for evil, but give thought to do what is honorable in the sight of all. If possible, so far as it depends on you, live peaceably with all. Beloved, never avenge yourselves, but leave it to the wrath of God, for it is written, "Vengeance is mine, I will repay, says the Lord."

Romans 12:17–19

The point of all this is you have to let it go. Forgiveness is not for them. It is for you to move on and keep your focus on the things of God, not the things of the world. If you focus on the anger, hurt, and pain someone caused you it pulls you away from the focus on what God has for you. You are being deceived by the enemy who is using that person or situation to get you off track.

I think of it this way; I am not going to let myself fall for the schemes and wickedness of the enemy so that I can be pulled away from the blessings and one true love of my existence. My relationship and love for God and my savior can never be outweighed or overtaken by sin. And if I am not receiving the answers to my prayers, it is on me and me alone. I am not going to be chumped into selling myself or my family or bloodline out of our rightful inheritance because the devil used someone to push my buttons. I will also fall back on my vow to pray twice as hard for that person to find the Lord and or repent for their mistakes.

God's rules and law will never change. He will never stray from it. So if I am praying and believing according to His Word, I can't lose. The only thing that stops me from receiving is letting sin in. Sin leads you OFF the path that is designed for you. Focus. Love God and yourself enough to learn and know what His Word says about and FOR you, and don't let offense from others pull you on to the loser track. Stay on the winning track—the God track. You are victorious. It is written and will NOT change as long as your heart is for God.

CHAPTER
32

"IF YOU'RE REAL GOD"

I know there are tons of people who just don't know. People who need answers and haven't been given direction or the truth. A lot of them want to know and turn to Him because they've heard of God or know what they have seen on TV or in passing conversations: "If you are real God, show yourself!"

It happens that sometimes, when you are at your lowest, or when you've hit the bottom of the barrel, or made that very last attempt for help, He speaks to you. It may not be in a loud audible, voice. It may not be with a major revelation that instantly changes your life trajectory. But it will be evident that He is speaking to you. He is reaching out to you to help you.

"But God shows his love for us in that while we were still sinners, Christ died for us" (Romans 5:8). "The LORD is near to the brokenhearted and saves the crushed in spirit" (Psalm 34:18).

I heard a woman give her testimony on a Christian news show I catch occasionally. She explained that her life had dropped down to a feeling of "nothingness". She prayed for help to God and felt that even He was not going to save her. She felt unloved and unworthy of anyone's love. She was miserable and ready to end her life to lose the pain and anguish she had been carrying for years. As she sat on her bed to take the bottle of pills to do the deed, she audibly heard a loud battle taking place above her head. The loud clanging of swords, she thought, and an evident struggle. She said she looked up and couldn't see a thing but heard it all the while. All of a sudden, it stopped and she felt as if a huge darkness had been lifted off of her, and there was a light and love penetrating her being. "For the Lord your God is he that goeth with you, to fight for you against your enemies, to save you" (Deuteronomy 20:4).

A very well-known pastor in the western part of the U.S. tells his story of how he had given in to the darkness of addiction and selling drugs to make ends meet and just not living right. He was out one night making a deal as he stood next to the driver's side window of a car and the deal went bad. The driver started driving off and opened fire on him. He saw the gun pointing straight at him and didn't have time to run or duck. Point blank, several shots rang out just a few feet from where he was standing. He knew he was hit. There was no way someone could miss that close. He did not have one bullet wound. He stated he dropped to his knees and knew without a doubt that God saved him.

Another man told a story about how he was struggling with bitterness and anger. He was sitting in his living room and dropped the TV remote. The channel clicked over to one of those TV preachers. The man tried changing the channel and it wouldn't change. He got up and tried on the TV as well. He changed the batteries in the remote. Nothing worked. So he sat. Then he listened to the preacher. The message was as if that preacher was speaking directly to him, he stated. The man said that the preacher spoke about how there was a man who had an issue with anger and bitterness. The preacher went on to explain the story that was exactly like the man with the remote. He heard about how the love and joy of the Lord can take all of that deep-seated pain away and wound up asking Jesus into his heart and life right there in his living room.

He will meet you where you are at. He knows you and you only need to invite Him in. "My frame was not hidden from You, When I was made in secret, *And* skillfully wrought in the lowest parts of the earth. Your eyes saw my substance, being yet unformed. And in Your book they all were written, The days fashioned for me, When *as yet there were* none of them" (Psalm 139:15–16).

CHAPTER 33

YOU GET WHAT YOU GO LOOKING FOR (BLESSINGS OR NOT?)

That leads me to a belief I have carried with me even before I knew the Lord. If you ask my children about the one thing I have impressed upon them that has stuck, it would be that you get what you go looking for in life. If you look for trouble, you will find it. If you look for a job (hard enough), you will find it. If you look for the answers, you will find them.

Life is quite a walk. There are highs, lows, ins, and outs. The direction you point yourself in and seek out has everything to do with your future. You seek out that which you desire, and if you desire to find the answers, you will. "Call to me and I will answer you and tell you great and unsearchable things you do not know" (Jeremiah 33:3).

In the same way, as you seek, you will find the truth. I am definitely not a person that listens to excuses. If you want the truth, you have to seek it out. If you want the blessings that the Lord has for you, you have to seek out His truth, study, investigate, listen, look, find it. It's not a hidden secret.

> If anyone teaches a different doctrine and does not agree with the sound words of our Lord Jesus Christ and the teaching that accords with godliness, he is puffed up with conceit and understands nothing. He has an unhealthy craving for controversy and for quarrels about words, which produce envy, dissension, slander, evil suspicions, and constant friction

among people who are depraved in mind and deprived of the truth, imagining that godliness is a means of gain.

1 Timothy 6:3–5

I have repeated several times that we have a manual for life. The Bible, the God-inspired, living, breathing, Word of God is our handbook or manual for life. Every story, every line, every example of situations we live and walk is written for our direction. What to do. What not to do. If you are looking for answers, get into the Word of God. The Holy Spirit will lead and guide you when you need that direction. Find yourself a Bible-based church to continue that growth and learning.

The truth is what you find when you get into the Word. Seek it. Look for the why, where, when, how. We all have questions. The answers are there for your review. The world has plenty of ways to trick you and keep you on the wrong track. "And no wonder, for even Satan disguises himself as an angel of light" (2 Corinthians 11:14).

Loving your children enough to teach and guide them is what you do as a good parent. You want them to grow into good people who are self-sufficient, productive, giving, and loving people. That guidance and discipline, that direction, is the foundation on which your children walk and grow. Our Father, our Creator, has given us the choice to walk and grow with that same foundation. He loves us with a love that is so untouchable here on earth. He wants us to live in joy and peace and with prosperity. Seek out the truth He gave us.

His Word is the seed that grows within us and protects, guides, and saves us from eternal death. Death is all around us and the way to life is through the Word of God. Seek the answers. Don't give in to the lies, deception, and trickery that pull you into thinking this is all unreal. Open your heart to the truth and you will find it. You get what you go looking for.

CHAPTER
34

WHY THE PERSECUTION?

The Word of God says that those who follow Him will be persecuted. John 15

> This is my command: Love each other. "If the world hates you, keep in mind that it hated me first. If you belonged to the world, it would love you as its own. As it is, you do not belong to the world, but I have chosen you out of the world. That is why the world hates you. Remember what I told you: 'A servant is not greater than his master.' If they persecute me, they will persecute you also. If they obeyed my teaching, they will obey yours also. They will treat you this way because of my name, for they do not know the one who sent me.
>
> John 15:17–21

There is a world full of people who hate Christians. We are called bigots and infidels and persecuted in horrific circumstances. Why do you think that is? There have been disagreements among men for generations. What is it that makes the Christian a full-blown target of some groups? Could it be that we are doing something right?

The Lord told us what was going to happen. Again, we have been targeted by the enemy because the Lord, our God, is truth and light and our Savior. The enemy, the devil, is jealous of us and hates us all. He has been scheming and using people for quite some time now. So deep and intense that there are whole religions out there with an underlying intent to kill off everyone that will not renounce Christ as their Savior. There are whole countries that have made it law that people are not to worship Christ and will be imprisoned if they do. Why do you suppose the world has such a hate for us? Where does that hate originate? Hmmm.

Let's consider this very strongly, shall we? Ponder this. I don't like several groups and their practices or their inability to respect others. But I certainly wouldn't entertain a practice where the main focus was to persecute them. The devil infiltrates people's minds, gets into the family unit, and focuses on molding and targeting the young, the old, and those who do not know the Lord. He uses them and causes chaos and hate to flourish.

I take it all as knowing that I am on the right path. When I am called a Bible thumper or holy roller or labeled as a kook, it makes me happy to know I represent my Lord and I shine with His love and intent. It is my mission to save as many people on this earth as I possibly can from eternal hell and damnation and pull them out of the clutches of the lies and hatred of the devil.

Remember, I've been in his presence. I know how much he hates us. You have the ability to fill yourself with the truth and knowledge and open yourself up to the reality of the lies fed to us on a daily basis.

Persecution? Yes. We may not be under the knife or in a country that bans Christianity, or maybe you are. If you are, I am praying protection around you as in 2 Kings and loose the archangels to cover you nonstop in Jesus' name. For me, I remember whose opinion is the one that matters. I don't live for man. I live for my Lord.

CHAPTER
35

THE ORDER (GOD, SPOUSE, KIDS)

I was married young. I was nineteen years old and going to be a mother. A "shotgun" wedding, I believe it was called. Things moved very quickly, and I relied heavily on my mother for answers to life's problems. I made some very poor choices back then, but I loved my mother and valued her opinions and believed what she said was right.

I wasn't aware of the real truth. Remember, I was raised a Catholic. I was a not-so-often church going kid and didn't know the Lord as I should have. I wasn't aware that God comes first in all things. Always.

In everything you do, put God first, and he will direct you and crown your efforts with success.

Proverbs 3:6

Jesus replied: "Love the Lord your God with all your heart and with all your soul and with all your mind."

Matthew 22:37

Since, then, you have been raised with Christ, set your hearts on things above, where Christ is, seated at the right hand of God. Set your minds on things above, not on earthly things. For you died, and your life is now hidden with Christ in God. When Christ, who is your life, appears, then you also will appear with him in glory.

Colossians 3:1–4

Exodus 20 tells us the following:

> And God spoke all these words: "I am the LORD your
> God, who brought you out of Egypt, out of the land
> of slavery. You shall have no other gods before me.
> You shall not make for yourself an image in the form
> of anything in heaven above or on the earth beneath
> or in the waters below. You shall not bow down to
> them or worship them; for I, the LORD your God,
> am a jealous God, punishing the children for the sin
> of the parents to the third and fourth generation of
> those who hate me, but showing love to a thousand
> generations of those who love me and keep my
> commandments."

The Lord clearly states that He is to be #1 in your life. He
said that we are not to idolize anything other than Him. That
means our spouse, children, money, work, or anything else. He
is to be our source, our main focus, day in and day out we are
to go to Him for all our needs. Not anyone or anywhere or to
anything else. After that we would have our spouse:

> But at the beginning of creation God "made them
> male and female." "For this reason a man will leave
> his father and mother and be united to his wife, and
> the two will become one flesh." So they are no longer
> two, but one flesh. Therefore what God has joined
> together, let no one separate.
>
> Mark 10:6–9

Without God we would not be here. We would have nothing. He is to be our everything. Then our spouse, and then our children.

CHAPTER
36

YOU CAN'T FOOL GOD

This chapter may not be for you, but it may be for someone very dear to you. So share it.

God loves you. Jesus. Loves. You. Whether you are gay, straight, black, white, yellow, orange, or believe you are a doorknob. You are loved. Whatever is going on inside your head, He knows. And get this—none of us are getting out of here alive.

You won't make it without Jesus. You need Him. You may not think you do. You may think you're all that and a bag of chips. But the truth is, without Jesus there is something missing. Life and the fire and light within you is not lit up. The purpose of your life walk isn't as strong and joyful as you want. You need Jesus.

I know this is very assuming of me to speak out about you, as I don't even know you. But really, I do. I have been you. I have been in the world. I know what it's like to live with love and happiness and still feel that lost feeling way down deep. And the reason is that you were created by an all-powerful, all-loving God. You were created by Him and for Him in His image.

The reason I know this is because I walk with Him daily. You have read about some experiences I have had, and believe me when I tell you there are thousands more. God has revealed Himself to me time and time again. I know who our God is, and I know my savior Jesus very well. I have a relationship with Him and talk with Him every day. There is so much fulfillment and joy in knowing how much I am loved. He never stops loving and protecting me. Jesus died on the Cross for me and for you and His sacrifice made it so we are able to receive all of the promises laid out in His Word.

The point is, He knows you, too. He created you and knows every hair on your head, every thought, mistake, and choice you have made. He has a plan for you that will take you to levels you have never thought for yourself. He wants you to be blessed and succeed. Every time you feel that gnawing or push to stop that bad choice or walk that different path, it is Him. He loves you with a love that is so intense and deep you would never want anything else if you only knew.

You will never fool Him. Living a life that feels off, living with choices and regret, living in fear and that unknowing feeling, living with remorse, heaviness, darkness, failure— these are all things He can take from you and more. The Word says: Jeremiah 17:9, "The heart is deceitful above all things, and desperately sick; who can understand it?" He knows your heart: "He said to them, 'You are the ones who justify yourselves in the eyes of others, but God knows your hearts. What people value highly is detestable in God's sight'" (Luke 16:15).

Give it to God. He is there for you to help you, lift you up, give you hope.

For I know the thoughts that I think toward you, says the Lord, thoughts of peace and not of evil, to give you a future and a hope.

Jeremiah 29:11

No temptation has overtaken you that is not common to man. God is faithful, and he will not let you be tempted beyond your ability, but with the temptation he will also provide the way of escape, that you may be able to endure.

1 Corinthians 10:13

Come to me, all who labor and are heavy laden, and I will give you rest.

Matthew 11:28

If you continue to look and seek Him out, He will provide for you, heal you, give you peace and joy, and help you when you walk through the fire. I may have already explained this, but it is worth repeating. My life is not always easy, but now that I live for the Lord instead of myself, I have the strength, wisdom, and guidance of a God who makes it known to me that I am loved and cared for no matter what I walk through. His strength is evident in my daily walk.

Know Him. Give Him your all. Be All-In. All-In-To-Win. There is no lukewarm. As a matter of fact, He wants your All or Nothing. "I know your deeds, that you are neither cold nor hot. I wish you were either one or the other! So, because you are lukewarm—neither hot nor cold—I am about to spit you out of my mouth" (Revelation 3:15–16).

Do not miss out on anything He has for you. I promise you won't regret it.

CHAPTER
37

DO YOU KNOW HOW TO GET TO HEAVEN?

If you die in your sleep tonight, do you know where you're going? Can you be 100 percent sure that you are going to make it to paradise? Are you 100 percent sure that you know there is or is not a spiritual world and afterlife when our bodies die? Is it that you need proof? What if you are wrong? What if you find out too late? That could be a very hot decision.

The people that hung Jesus on the Cross wanted proof. They had proof in their faces and refused to accept it. The truth was too hard for them to take in and believe. Their generations spent thousands of years waiting for the foretold Messiah to arrive, and when He did, they spat in his face and didn't listen. Don't be a rerun of those wholly documented and very disturbingly mistaken people.

Mohammed didn't die for you. Buddha didn't die for you—he even said he didn't want to be idolized. Mecca isn't going to save you. Crystals, spells, the moon and stars, aliens, Jupiter, Venus, Shiva, Vishnu, and whoever else is out there will not to save you. There is one true God and Creator. There is one true Savior, and the only way to salvation (paradise-life after death) is through Jesus. Ask Him into your heart now before it's too late. What do you have to lose? Or what is it you think you will lose? I lost nothing. I gained tremendously.

Repeat out loud from your heart:

"Lord, I am sorry for my sins. I believe You sent Jesus as a sacrifice to die on the Cross to save me from sin and death and You raised Him from the dead. Jesus, come into my heart and be my Savior."

There are so many choices you can make in life. This one is, by far, the most important and life- altering change you can ever make. Don't waste one more minute in an uncertain world with an uncertain future. Choose life and live it to the absolute fullest. Live with and serve our Savior to be fully blessed and walk in abundance in every area of your life.

Blessings and all my love to you.

CHRISTIAN TERMS:

Receive It – grab hold of, take it.

Manifest – brought forth into your presence or life.

Believing For It – Absolutely believing the Lord will provide your specific request.

Standing On – firmly planted on a scripture or word or belief from the Lord.

One Accord – all together, on the same page, in one unified belief.

Mantle – A special gifting or ability from God.

Confirmation – a word or message that reiterates or confirms a prayer or word you felt you received from the Lord.

Condemnation – of feeling of dread or wrongdoing that is not from the Lord.

Conviction – The Lord prompting you to stop it or correct that wrong doing.

Unction – that prompting or notion, a feeling inside warning or telling you something.

Repent – to turn around.

Milton Keynes UK
Ingram Content Group UK Ltd.
UKHW020234301123
433483UK00016B/925